I0821835

# My Husband the Poet

**My Husband the Poet**


Printed in Seoul, Korea

First Published in August 2006
By Seoul Selection
B1 Korean Publishers Association Bldg., 105-2 Sagan-dong, Jongno-gu, Seoul 110-190, Korea
Tel 82-2-734-9567/8
Fax 82-2-734-9562
www.seoulselection.com



ISBN 89-91913-07-5 03040

# My Husband the Poet

by

Mok Sun-ok

The wife of the poet Ch'ŏn Sang-pyŏng

Translated by Brother Anthony of Taizé

# Contents

# The Translator's Preface

Early May, 1993. The first time I visited the little café called Kwich'ŏn, hidden down an alley in Seoul's Insa-dong, and met Mok Sun-Ok, I had no idea of the relationship that was beginning. I did not at first realize the link between the café and a brief note I had read in a newspaper a few days earlier, announcing the death of the poet Ch'ŏn Sang-pyŏng. A cassette was playing some rather solemn music, one of Bach's Cello Sonatas, I recall, alternating with a Korean folk-singer's melancholy version of what I later learned was the poem 'Kwich'ŏn.' Yet Mok Sun-Ok's smile was bright as she welcomed us, and served me my first cup of *Mogwa-ch'a,* her famous quince tea. Slowly, during the weeks and months that followed, I learned more about the poet and his wife.

That was more than a dozen years ago. The old Kwich'ŏn café has been demolished. At present there are two new Kwich'ŏn cafés and we have all grown that much older. In the meantime, almost every year I have joined the crowd of friends who go up to the hillside cemetery just outside of Seoul to pay our respects before Ch'ŏn Sang-pyŏng's grave on April 28, his death anniversary. I have translated his poems and they have been published in the United States, and in Korea. Translations into other languages have followed – French, Spanish, German, Romanian . . . I have drunk countless cups of quince tea in Kwich'ŏn, to say nothing of *Yuja-ch'a* citron tea, and other teas, too.

I have taken quite a few people to Kwich'ŏn in that time and told them the story of the poet and his wife, shown them the poem that gave its name to the café, introduced them to Mok Sun-Ok. If they were Korean, they could then talk with her while I relaxed. But many were from other countries, and she only speaks Korean! So the idea came of translating this book, published soon after the poet's death.

Smiles can speak volumes, of course. And they do, especially when the visitors have heard some of the story – her childhood in Hiroshima, the death of her father somewhere in the city center when the atom bomb exploded on August 6, 1945, her early meetings with her brother's friend Ch'ŏn Sang-pyŏng. It does not take long to relate his arrest and torture in 1968, the broken health that led him to write the poem 'Kwich'ŏn' in 1970, thinking that he would soon die, and his sudden disappearance the following year. When his friends published a memorial collection of his poems, a phone call from the municipal asylum told them he was not dead, but confined there, very sick.

So Mok Sun-Ok became the broken poet's wife, his caring companion for the next twenty years. Together, they experienced almost unimaginable poverty, moving into a succession of increasingly tiny rented rooms. Sometimes they could only afford a single block of dried *ra-*

*myŏn* noodles for the two of them! She endured his impatience and strange behavior, understanding that he had never really lost his childhood innocence. It was not until 1985, when she was able to open her tiny café in Insa-dong, that a little money became available beyond what he might earn for an occasional poem. After keeping him company through the last years of increased weakness, she became the devoted guardian of his memory. Often, friends comment: 'Most poets are forgotten once they're dead. It's only Ch'ŏn who's much better known now than in his lifetime. Thanks to his wife!'

This book is her way of telling their story. It is told as she lived it, very simply, without any attempt to make things sound easy when they were hard. But she makes no fuss, when other people would make a lot of fuss. So I have translated it, because there are people outside of Korea who ought to be able to read it. This is a very Korean voice, recording some very Korean experiences in a truly Korean way. It is really quite a story!

Thanks to her efforts, there are memorials to Ch'ŏn Sang-pyŏng in various parts of Korea, stones inscribed with one of his poems. Here and there, memorial events are organized, cultural festivals bearing his name are held, memorial halls have been built, and each year a Korean poet is awarded the 'Ch'ŏn Sang-pyŏng Literary Award.' Meanwhile, Mok Sun-Ok ensures that there is never a day when the door of Kwich'ŏn café stays shut. For she sees the people coming as part of her family, not as customers, and it would be too unkind if someone came, having nowhere else to go, and found the door shut.

Translating her book is my way of saying a quiet

'Thank-you' for the tea and the welcome, all the moments shared during these years. I am more than grateful to have become part of the Kwich'ŏn family. I hope that people reading these pages will come to understand why Ch'ŏn Sang-pyŏng could inspire such loving friendship in so many people, and why I feel we owe so much to Mok Sun-Ok. *Samonim, komapsŭmnida.*

Brother Anthony

# Tomb with dandelions

It was wonderful! While he was alive, my husband had so many friends. He would sit happily with someone he had just met, repeating over and over again, '*Yonoma, yonoma,* you lovely fellow, you,' and he only had to set eyes on a pretty girl to fall in love with her on the spot.

In the years before he died, he used to come down into central Seoul twice every week, on Wednesdays and Fridays. Dropping into Kwich'ŏn, the tea-shop that I run in the Insa-dong neighborhood, or into some other coffee-shop, he would meet old acquaintances or make new ones; those were the happiest moments in his weekly program. But now his 'outing to this world,' as he called life in the poem '*Kwich'ŏn*' (Back to Heaven), is over.

Soon after his funeral, I began to get the impression that my husband, in going back to heaven, had transferred his affections from people to flowers. Whenever I visited his hillside grave in the municipal cemetery in Ŭijŏngbu, just outside Seoul, I was amazed to see how many flowers were growing in the grass around it: humble, short-stemmed dandelions fluttering their yellow heads lightly in the early summer breeze, here and there a solitary purple thistle flourishing, while cosmos and balsam quietly awaited their turn to bloom. The sight of them, growing freely yet all in perfect harmony, reminded me of the tiny flower-bed in front of our house, they looked so homely.

True, on the day of the funeral the pear blossom in the orchard just below the cemetery was at its height and the sight of those trees all covered in white had impressed the mourners deeply, but the masses of flowers we found decorating the grass round the grave when we went there to mark the forty-ninth day after his death made everyone exclaim. Their beauty brought comfort to us, for our hearts had been saddened by the final departure of my husband, the poet Ch'ŏn Sang-pyŏng.

A little later I learned that all that abundance of wild flowers was not the result of mere chance. A few days after we had celebrated the forty-ninth day, when I went to visit the grave alone, I found a young man examining the ground. As we exchanged a few words, I discovered that the cosmos and balsam were gifts from him, a token of his sympathy. He explained that he was a university student living on Yoido Island, in the center of Seoul, and that he loved reading Ch'ŏn Sang-pyŏng's poems. He had planted the seedlings a few days after the funeral and had come back today because he was curious to see how they were growing.

For a moment I was at a loss for words, overwhelmed with gratitude. I seemed to hear my husband's happy voice ringing in my ears: 'You see, wife. Just look how many people know me. It's great to be a poet.'

While he was alive, people were drawn to him either because of the way his poems touched them, so simply and directly, or because they liked the perfect innocence of the man himself, the way he lived without any attachments or desires. Old friends and fellow writers, neighbors in Insa-dong where Kwich'ŏn is located, families and individuals living near our home in Ŭijŏngbu: there were so many people who were concerned about him and looked after him. The flowers blossoming around his grave seemed to show that the same affection would continue to surround him now he was dead, and I could not help feeling deeply moved.

He left this world on April 28, 1993. Since then, time has flown like an arrow, as we say, rushing by like a stream, and I have had little chance to miss him. In fact I have deliberately tried not to miss him. In an effort to prevent there being any spare moments in which to feel the pain, I have kept myself as busy as before, trying to cope.

In the twenty-two years of our married life, there was never once an occasion when we spent any time apart. We were always side by side, at home or outside, and I never once felt that I was alone. Perhaps that is why now I often have the feeling that he is nearby. I still hear the raucous voice with which he invariably greeted every customer entering Kwich'ŏn if he happened to be sitting there: 'Come on in! There's room, there's room.'

Late in the evening, after I have locked up and am sitting in the bus going home, I always have a feeling I must hurry, although there is no reason. It must be because I am thinking of how he was always waiting impatiently for me to arrive.

'*Mundunga*, how come you're so late? Now tell me, who came today; how many customers did you have?' His eyes in the photo hanging in my room seem to be questioning me, and I find myself explaining that the bus was held up in the traffic, and telling how this and that person dropped in.

The man whose hair I combed and whose feet I washed every day has gone, and my sense of loss is greater than anyone can imagine. I only now realize how painful it is to miss someone, when you can no longer physically touch them to make sure they are there. When the photograph is not sufficient to quiet my heart, I go up to where he is buried. I try to comfort myself: 'After all, he lived another five years. You ought to be grateful for that much.'

Back in 1988, my husband was at death's door with acute cirrhosis of the liver. His stomach had swollen up until he looked like a pregnant mother at term, and the constant diarrhoea meant we had to change him dozens of times a day. The prognosis was grave, the doctor had told me that death was certain, and I was trembling before the impending blow.

The doctor cast apologetic glances at the people around: 'It looks as if it's the end.' He urged me to prepare for the worst, and comforted me. But then a doctor friend of ours arranged for him to be admitted to his clinic in the provincial city of Ch'unch'on and I began to think that we couldn't just let him die like that. For the next five months I was at the mercy of his sickness as I made daily journeys from Seoul to Ch'unch'ŏn, then from Ch'unch'ŏn back to Seoul, not once missing a single day.

Going to and fro in the bus, and sitting late at night in the hospital room, I would secretly cry as I prayed: 'God, please let our Ch'ŏn Sang-pyŏng live another five years! Only five more years!' I have no idea why I asked for five years. I simply said whatever came into my mind.

Perhaps that was what did it. Anyway, the day came when my husband, who had been given just a week to live, walked out of the hospital on his way home. On that day I felt that everything in the whole world was mine.

The years passed. 1993 was the fifth year. My husband entered the world beyond as if he had suddenly found himself out in the fields at nightfall and gone hurrying home. All through the previous winter he had stayed indoors, from October onwards. First he was too poorly, then the weather was too cold for him to venture out. He said he would start coming down to Kwich'ŏn again once the warm days of May arrived. But in the end he made his eternal journey 'Back to Heaven' just a few days before May came. We who were left behind felt all the more regret on that account, but now I am sure that is not what he would have wanted:

I'll go back to heaven again.
Hand in hand with the dew
that melts at a touch of the dawning day,

I'll go back to heaven again.
With the dusk, together, just we two,
at a sign from a cloud after playing on the slopes

I'll go back to heaven again.
At the end of my outing to this beautiful world,
I'll go back and say: That was beautiful. . . .

I only have to read that poem *'Kwich'ŏn'* (Back to Heaven) inscribed on the back of the stone beside his grave, and I feel comforted. My husband always considered life in this world as an outing from heaven. As he said, now he has finished his outing and, after staying here for a while, has gone back home to heaven.

If people find that I provided him with at least a little chance to live freely and happily while he was here, then I will have no cause to be ashamed of my life either. Rather we comfort each other, when I consider how my outing was so satisfying because I spent my whole lifetime in the company of a man who lived in such utter authenticity.

The road we travelled in the course of our outing, with me supporting him as we advanced hand in hand, was not always so splendid and did not by any means lie smooth. There was a constant icy wind and sometimes it was like a winter road at sunset with flurries of sleet blowing across it. It was certainly no pretty, gently winding lane where you can always stop and quietly rest for a bit before going on, of the kind open to anyone with just a modicum of human affection.

I want to tell you about the many footprints that

mark the road we took together. I will be talking about Ch'ŏn Sang-pyŏng the poet, certainly, but there will be footprints of mine too, as I tell you how I lived as the wife of Ch'ŏn Sang-pyŏng the man.

# His watch

'What's the date today?'

'What time is it?'

'Is the weather cloudy or bright?'

He always started the day with questions like that.

Eight o'clock. That was his rising time, and I had orders to wake him up, even if it meant slapping his face, if he did not wake by himself.

Once up, the first thing was a cigarette, then a pee. Next came the turning on of radio or television to listen to music and the news. I had already had breakfast and now was the time for me to come into the room with a basin of water to wash his face and hands.

While I was doing that, the radio or television would be delivering an endless flow of information about the day's weather, the date, the precise time, and so on, to all of which he would listen intently. Yet still he could not absorb it. He would only feel certain after he had asked me again, just to make sure, and once I had left to go to work, he would keep asking my mother the same questions over and over again.

He never for one moment took off his watch in the

course of the year, not once in twelve months. He even wore it while he slept.

He was for ever boasting that his watch told exactly the same time as the clock on the television, but he was all the time on edge with his systematic efforts to make sure it never varied so much as a minute, a second even, from that precise electric timepiece. His watch always told the right time, but when it came to checking its accuracy he needed my collaboration, and my mother's too.

'What time is it now?'

From the moment he opened his eyes in the morning until he fell asleep late in the evening, he was constantly asking the same question. Sometimes he would wake up early. In that case, although he was wearing his watch, he would invariably wake me up, no matter how deeply I was asleep, to ask what time it was.

'It's only five o'clock. It's much too early. Go back to sleep.'

'Ah, alright.'

Then he would seem reassured, satisfied, and settle down to go back to sleep as he spoke.

Looking straight at a calendar, he would ask, 'What's the date today?' and consulting his watch, 'What time is it?' so there were times when mother and I would tease him for his constant questioning by giving off-beat answers.

'*Ŏmma-yo*, how many minutes past the hour is it?'

'Well, I don't rightly know. It must be ten past, surely?'

'No, it's seven minutes past!'

'Then why ask me, if you already know?'

'I wanted to see if your watch and mine told the same time. My watch tells the same time as the television.'

'My watch is the same, too.'

'Not at all. It's wrong!'

For us it was funny, but he was always completely serious about checking the time. And he would always get up, eat, have a drink, smoke a cigarette, and go to sleep, according to the precise time told by his electric watch.

He was convinced that so long as he lived a steady life, God would not punish him and he would not fall sick again.

According to his timetable, the right time for the morning meal was precisely eleven o'clock. Moreover, he would never eat anything at all until it was time for his morning meal, that was a combination of breakfast and lunch. Instead, as eleven approached, he would keep telling mother what time it was. It was like a control tower embarked on a countdown before the launch of an artificial satellite.

'*Ŏmma-yo*, it's a quarter to . . .'

'*Ŏmma-yo*, it's five to.'

Then and only then, at eleven precisely and not a minute before, would he let us serve the meal. If mother brought in the food a few minutes early, he would pay no attention to it until the time was right. He would protest: 'I only eat when it's eleven, that's the right time for me to eat, why are you in such a rush?' and he would wait until it was eleven.

With such a son-in-law, Mother would sometimes play a joke. If she pretended not to hear when he announced 'quarter to' and 'ten to' he would become terribly agitated. Then, as he announced 'five to' a veritable little squabble would arise between them.

'*Ŏmma-yo,* it's five to.'

'I must hurry up and serve.'

'You see, if I hadn't told you, it would have been terrible.'

'But everything's ready, I only have to serve it up. What on earth do you mean, terrible?'

'Still, it's as I say. If I hadn't told you, it would have been terrible! Why don't you wear a watch? I bought you one, why won't you wear it? You have to look at your watch. Your watch. If you don't keep your eye on the time . . . If I hadn't told you, that would have been terrible.'

He would keep repeating, 'That would have been terrible,' with an artless air that was so comic, mother found herself forced to laugh, although it was something that was always happening.

Sometimes he would take a snooze before the morning meal, and that too always gave rise to an altercation. If he happened to have woken up a bit earlier than usual, he would be drowsy. In which case he would start: 'I mustn't fall asleep, must I *Ŏmma-yo*? I mustn't fall asleep.'

He would repeat the same thing over and over again. He was worried he might not be on time for his meal.

'Go to sleep. If you're still asleep at five to eleven, I'll wake you up in time for your meal. Sleep now.'

'You won't forget? If I doze off, I may be sound asleep.'

'You've got two hours yet; stop worrying.'

Once he had been through the formalities of obtaining Mother's reassurance, he would go to sleep. Then sometimes he would open his eyes at exactly five to eleven, without having been called. In that case, he would immediately turn on Mother.

'Why, *Ŏmma*, you nearly didn't wake me up! If I'm asleep, you must wake me up, even if it means slapping my face. You were going to forget, if I hadn't woken up first, weren't you?'

'Have I ever not woken you up? I'll give you your meal when it strikes eleven.'

No matter what Mother said or did, there was no end to his ceaseless lament of 'That would have been terrible.'

He ate twice a day. His evening meal at nine was taken care of by my niece Yŏng-jin. She loved her uncle as dearly as if she had been his real daughter, and would always prepare dishes he liked as well as keep him company, so that his evenings were spent happily.

By the time I closed Kwich'ŏn and got home, it was usually past eleven o'clock. From then until bedtime at twelve forty, I was all the time obliged to give precise answers to the question, 'What time is it now?' He had decided on twelve forty as his regular bedtime; prior to that I had the task of bringing about a favorable atmosphere to help sleep to come.

At midnight, I would turn off the television and switch on the radio, because we listened to music before going to sleep. Then at twelve forty I would turn off the radio and change the thirty watt light-bulb for a ten watt one, that stayed burning while he slept. Once he was lying down and I had finally arranged the coverlet over him, his timetable for the day had been successfully completed.

'No matter what happens, be sure to come into my room at midnight. The radio has to be turned on.'

'You're sure you know the radio has to go off at twelve forty?'

With those words he always made me responsible for the proper completion of his daily routine, and I did my best to be punctual to the minute.

# 'Forgive me just this once. . .'

His stubborn concern with precision was not limited to the timetable. The amount he ate, his habits, every aspect of life had to be as regular and unvarying as a line drawn with a ruler.

If ever he failed to observe some point precisely, he would get angry and keep on at me or my mother, scolding us. He was for ever checking and rechecking whether he was keeping the rules he had freely laid down for himself. It was a kind of obsession. There was no end to his efforts to live without an inch of leeway.

His eleven o'clock meal was one example. Besides the food, there absolutely had to be two small bottles of beer on the table. The first bottle would be drunk in two stages, one glass during the meal and the second thirty minutes after the end of the meal. The other bottle he drank at three in the afternoon.

Then the quantity he quaffed at any one time was precisely fixed too. When he poured the beer into the glass, the top inch or so had to be left empty. If he drank from a glass that was full to the brim, he felt he was drinking too much.

After he had poured out two such glasses from a small bottle, there was still some beer left but he categorically refused to drink that. He used to say that if he drank the beer that was left over, God would surely punish him.

He was afraid that if he drank too much, he might fall sick with cirrhosis again as before. He used to recall the mountainous distended stomach he had at that time, and would stroke his belly as if to say it might swell up again if he drank too much.

Sometimes there was an exception. But in that case he would never drink more without permission, following the proper procedure and getting my agreement first, before he drank.

If he got bored in the later part of the afternoon after three o'clock, or if his thoughts kept wandering, or if he had written a poem, or wanted to write one, his mind often seemed to turn to thoughts of a drink. In which case he would look to mother for help.

'*Ŏmma,* I'll pay you back later, if you'll just let me have one more bottle.' He knew that the invariable reply would come: 'Only if Yŏng-jin gets her aunt's permission.' Then a phone call would be made to me down at Kwich'ŏn.

'Have you had lunch?'

'Yes, of course.'

'Look. Forgive me just this once. . .'

'What is there to forgive?'

'I mean, I'm desperate.'

I knew what he meant, but I would deliberately pretend not to and he would explain the problem:

'Forgive me just this once. . .'

'I want to drink one more bottle of beer. Do forgive me, please.'

'So you're so much in need of a drink? But only today. It mustn't happen again.'

'Of course not. I don't usually do this, do I? Not every day?'

'Alright. Another time you must go without, though.'

'Right. Right. Thank ye. Thank ye. I'll just put *Ŏmma* on the line.'

Then when mother took the phone, I would duly tell her: 'Let him have one more bottle,' so concluding the process of ensuring that he had my permission.

The reasons he advanced were always the same.

'I'm just stuck here at home and I don't feel very cheerful today.' 'I want to write a poem and I reckon it will take some more beer if I'm to write properly.' 'I've just finished a poem and I feel like drinking one more bottle.' And so on. And I would always pretend to be taken in by the promise of 'Only this once.'

Once in a while mother happened not to be at home when he was longing for an extra drink. He would look outside to see if he could see her and if he failed, I would receive a phone call: 'Is it alright if I go out for a while?'

He was so unsteady on his feet, I was afraid he would fall down; I would answer, 'Wait just a bit.' At which he would obediently wait until mother came back, when I would get the usual phone call asking me to forgive him.

It was not only drink; cigarettes, too, were precisely regulated. He got through one pack a day, but time was the main factor. At the start of half an hour he would smoke half of one cigarette, then extinguish it, lighting up again and smoking the second half in the second half hour. If ever he dozed off and passed the allotted time, the remaining portion was duly thrown away unsmoked. 'One cigarette an hour,' was the ratio he insisted on observing. As a result, he always knew at once if someone had filched one of his cigarettes and would start to complain that one had disappeared.

Even when he had all the beer and cigarettes he needed for the moment, he always liked to have a certain quantity of each near him in reserve. If only one or two packs of cigarettes were left, he would phone me: 'You'd better bring some cigarettes when you come.' Then a little later he would call again to see if I'd got them. He would only be reassured when I came home and put the cigarettes in their proper place.

With beer it was the same. If there was only one bottle on the table with his meal, there was trouble, he would start to shout. Mother might insist: 'I'll get the bottle you drink in the afternoon a bit later on,' it was no use. 'Go and buy it now! Buy it now!' He would insist.

The family knew what he was like and only had to conform for everything to be alright but there were times when uninformed visitors got bitterly insulted. Once some guests turned up with canned beer. They must have been told, 'Ch'ŏn Sang-pyŏng likes beer.' The problem was that he would only drink bottled beer, and refused absolutely to drink canned beer, even though the contents were the same. He demanded that they take it back and get bottles in exchange.

'Forgive me just this once. . .'

Mother was embarrassed and protested: 'Is that any way to treat visitors?' At which he got furious and started to shout.

'No. I won't drink it. I won't. Take it out and throw it away, go on!'

Anyone learning that the containers in which it was packed were the reason for those shouted commands to take perfectly good beer and throw it away, would surely have laughed. He was different. He absolutely refused to touch canned beer, and would only drink the bottled kind. That was his Ch'ŏn Sang-pyŏng kind of obstinacy.

One day a young couple came all the way up from Ch'angwŏn, in the far south of the country, to visit him. They were fans of his and had taken a day off from work to come and see the poet in person. First they called in at the cafe and drank a cup of tea, then we went out for lunch before I sent them up to the house. It all took time and it was three or four o'clock by the time they reached Ŭijŏngbu. They had taken some photos and were chatting when he suddenly asked:

'When are you leaving?'

'We're taking the evening train.'

He looked startled and began urging them to be off quickly, over and over again. Mother, who had been preparing to give them supper before they left, tried to calm him down but he would hear none of it.

'You must go quickly. You'll be too late. Go quickly. At once. You must.'

Seeing there was no way to overcome his anxiety, the two of them left hurriedly, without any supper. The reason for his insistence was simply that he felt it would take them hours to get to Seoul station; they might be late and miss the train.

When the young couple arrived at Seoul station and phoned me at Kwich'ŏn, all I could do was apologize on his behalf. I still feel grateful to them for understanding him, though he shooed them off without letting them eat; they even sent us copies of the snapshots later on.

He was already past sixty but he spent every day of his last years living like a model schoolboy, keeping all the rules. As befits the wife of a model schoolboy, I began to respect the dictates of his electric watch. I might be fed up with his rigid insistence on 'keeping time,' inwardly I admired him for it.

Frankly, it was a habit that was hard for ordinary mortals to follow. He would act like a child and all the time insisted on having his own way, but deep down there was a fundamental innocence.

If I never once found his strict punctuality or his special style of obstinacy hard to bear, it was surely because I had decided to marry him on account of his frailty, of a concern that he would vanish at a touch, because he had the purity of a child and no one to turn to.

## Always on the move

The house we lived in for the last years of his life was at the foot of Mount Surak. The address says Changam village in Ŭijŏngbu but it lies right up against the boundary with Seoul, it's like being in Seoul. Strictly speaking, it's the house where my mother used to live with my elder brother. When he died in 1985, we moved in with her, more than eight years ago at the time of writing.

The house lies down a cul-de-sac in a rural hamlet set in the midst of fields and nursery-gardens. The rooms are tiny and dark, no better than those you can rent in any squatters' area, but he used to love it.

Once he published an essay about the house, entitled 'The Place Where I Live,' where he wrote:

> No matter how hard it rains, I never have to worry about water. Our house has a clean underground source of drinking water. The garden is thick with greenery, it's really a fine sight.

For years after we got married, we lived in a succession of rented rooms, experiencing all kinds of difficulties and hardships. After coming to live in this house I was at last able to feel a sense of peace. His body has left here now, but since his grave is not far away, I often think that he must feel a similar peace.

He may not have made much of a success of his life, and he had no great reserves of energy, still he was not insensitive to poverty. That becomes clear if you see how, although he was an onlooker on the sidelines of life, he several times celebrated his poverty in poems with real sensitivity.

Just after our wedding, he wrote a poem called 'My house.' It was a quite astonishing way of approaching the normal duty of a husband newly saddled with a wife to provide a home for them to live in:

> Won't somebody give me a house? I roar to the heavens. Hear me, someone, to the ends of the earth. . . I got married just a few weeks ago, so how can I help but shout like this? God in his heaven will hear with a smile. ( . . .) So I'm shouting like a giant. A house is a treasure. The whole world may crumble and fall, my house will remain.

What hope was there of ever getting 'my house'? None at all. After our wedding, the first place we went to live in was a thatched house in Sangye-dong, on the north-eastern outskirts of Seoul. There we got a room with a bit of kitchen space and began our married life. It meant making a deposit of fifty thousand Won and paying five thousand Won each month in rent. In those days, the usual sum people offered as a wedding present was five hundred or a thousand Won. We received a total of a hundred and twenty thousand Won at our wedding.

That little house huddling low at the foot of Mount Surak was a joy to live in, mainly because of the perfectly clean air. After a year we had to move because the owner's younger sister was coming to live there. No other room being available in that neighborhood, we found ourselves renting a room down closer to the bus terminal.

Our next home was a real beehive, with no less than twelve families living in it. There were twelve rooms in all. The owner lived in one, each of the other eleven was rented out to a separate family. Except for us, every room had two or three babies; there was a constant clamor, all uproar and confusion. The children made a racket, the grown-ups made a racket. We had no children, but I had a husband who made more noise than any child.

We lived in that house for seven years. At first it cost two hundred thousand Won deposit with twenty thousand Won rent, and we managed alright as that increased to three hundred thousand, then three hundred and fifty. At that point we were unable to pay the rent for two months running and were told to get out. We'd been there nearly ten years, but all the ties accumulated in that time melted in a flash like so much froth. The owner was unsympathetic, we had no choice but to leave. Helpless people are bound to lose out, so I set about packing. Our total belongings amounted to one cabinet and my husband's books.

When I had finished packing everything, I found him sitting on a swing out in the yard. The swing stood in the very middle of the spacious yard and he often used to play there with the children from the next room. He was already forty-three years old.

We lived for a long time in that 'twelve families under one roof' house and inevitably, with so many different families living together, there were any number of unforgettable incidents.

Once a couple with two children moved in. The wife was over-sensitive to questions of money, perhaps because they had known such grinding poverty that she had been affected by it.

'There's no light bulb in our kitchen, why do we have to pay the same electricity charge as the owners when they have a bulb in theirs?' 'Our kids don't use the privy to shit. Only my husband and I do; so why do we have to pay the same charge for emptying it as families where five or six people go to shit?'

She was so determined not to be diddled out of so much as a single eyelash, she calculated every last penny. Of course, in mathematical terms she was quite right. Her desire to save even just a few Won, insignificant though it might seem to others, could be considered perfectly natural in someone so poor.

Still, what a way to live! Normally, if we suffer some loss we can be sure that a greater gain will follow; her shrivelled heart seemed unable to allow itself that degree of freedom.

Perhaps out of irritation, the owner's wife suddenly awarded us the title of 'model household.'

'The people in the room next to yours have been living here for seven years now, and I've never heard talk like that from them. Why do you go on like that? If you're going to be so penny-pinching, you can move out.'

The woman was not to be outdone, though. With a mere, 'Give me my money back,' she packed their things and they moved on after spending a bare three weeks there.

Later, we got a light installed in our kitchen too. Since there were only the two of us, we used far less of everything than any of the other families, yet we paid exactly the same share of the household expenses without so much as a murmur. The light in the kitchen came as a kind of belated reward.

'But of course my husband always makes a lot of noise instead.'

The landlord fixed the light himself, while stressing how extraordinary a thing it was. He was even kind enough to add that now we might turn on the light in the kitchen sometimes. Yet only a little later we had to pack up our things. Overnight the owners' kindness turned into downright cruelty, all on account of unpaid rent.

The best thing about that house was the way people could make as much noise as they liked, no one ever showed a sign of being vexed. No matter how much of a racket the kids made, the owners never interfered, and the same was true of the tenants.

People used to get worried if my husband made an effort to be quiet, when usually he bellowed like an ox. They would ask, 'Why, is he sick?' They had grown so accustomed to hearing him bellowing night and day.

The place where we unpacked our belongings for the third time was more like a storeroom, not what you would call a house at all. Situated in a shanty-town up in Ŭijŏngbu, the deposit was a hundred and fifty thousand Won, the monthly rent fifteen thousand. The main consolation was that it was right beside the house where my mother and brother were living.

Goodness knows how much poisonous coal-gas we inhaled from the coal briquettes we burned in that house. No matter how careful we were, the kitchen was directly connected to the room itself, so there was no way we could keep the fumes out, short of a complete rebuild.

We were in a daily state of asphyxiation from the fumes, I reckon any normal human being would have died; once I lost consciousness. Fortunately, my niece Yŏng-jin discovered what had happened early in the morning and took emergency measures, so nothing disastrous happened.

I got into the habit, as soon as I woke up, of dashing outside and breathing the pure air. Oddly enough, while I developed a positive neurosis about the fumes, my husband was completely unaffected and remained in good health.

Having several times survived the threat of death in this way allowed me to feel how tight my hold on life was. The fumes acted as messengers from the world beyond during the winter, then in the summer monsoons I had to suffer hell from flooding.

I shall never forget the woman from the next room that I used to bail out the rain water with, if only because she was the first person we fought with on moving into our new quarters.

There was no landlord in the house, only tramps like us lived there. The owner lived in a house nearby, at the back of a tiny store, so that we were just four families, all accustomed to living in rented rooms.

Then for some unknown reason this woman, known as 'Kyongae's mother,' who lived in the biggest room, started to act as if she was in charge. She was one year younger than I was, and she intervened in the other families' lives in all kinds of ways. If the children in the next room cried, she would complain of the noise. If she saw any of the men drunk, she would stand scowling and threaten to report them for disturbing the peace. She would praise her own husband to the skies, he was 'like an angel,' while she was all the time cursing the men in the other rooms as good-for-nothing louts.

Once I came back after going down to Pusan alone for a memorial ceremony in my husband's family. I was only away for one day, but I found the paper covering the fretwork door to our room all pierced with black holes. I always worried in case he dropped a lighted cigarette and started a fire, so I felt my heart begin to beat fast.

'Has there been a fire?'

'Not at all!'

He said nothing more. It was only when I went to tell mother I was back that I heard the whole story.

'My goodness, what a to-do! I'm all turned up inside. Do you know, that woman and he had a fight. Then she took a coal briquette from the hearth, while it was still burning, and threw it into your room. Why, if I'd been younger, I'd have at least smeared their room with a turd.'

She advised me to pretend to know nothing, but I felt

obliged to ask him more details. It had all started with a rude expression he had used. If any of the women failed to turn off the communal tap after getting water, he would do it instead, muttering as he did so, '*Ssangnyŏnŭi Kashina*, Bloody bitch.' Then, as he went back to the kitchen, he would scold them, 'You mustn't waste water.'

If any one protested: 'What earthly difference does it make if we waste water or not?' he would swear some more: 'Bloody bitches!' Actually, the expression was not really an oath at all, it was just a habit his lips had got into; but at last it had got him into trouble.

Kyongae's mother had drawn some water and failed to turn off the tap, at which the usual curse must have emerged from his lips. With her fiery temperament, she wasn't going to let that pass. She slid back the kitchen door and started a slanging match in which he gave as good as he got.

'You cur!'

'You bitch!'

'What did you call me? You son of a cur!'

'You frog-faced hag! You hog-faced hag!'

The woman, who was on the plump side, heard him up to that point, then suddenly turned and stormed out. She came back with a still-glowing briquette that she hurled into the room. Goodness knows what would have happened, if the student couple in the next room hadn't put an end to the quarrel.

On hearing of it all, my heart began to pound. Who ever heard of anyone throwing lumps of burning coal into a room where they know someone is sitting? I wanted to go rushing out and set about her. I wanted to ask her if she really didn't know that there was no scrap of harm in him, that he just raised his voice and spat out a few oaths sometimes from force of habit, nothing more. There's a proper time for fighting. Only I'm nothing for confrontations and incapable of making a scene. My job now was to smooth down the two of them after their quarrel.

'You frog-faced hag' was his worst oath; if he had gone so far as to use it, it meant he must have been really upset.

'Running after me swearing like that! You expect me to keep quiet?'

'I know. It's alright.'

After first taking care of my husband, who had still not calmed down, I called on Kyongae's mother and apologized. I explained that it was simply the way he was, and asked her to understand.

A few months went past. She was for ever scolding the children, nagging the other tenants, and generally acting as if it was her house. It was difficult enough, living in hardship in such cramped conditions, I had no talent for putting up with some crazy woman intent on making trouble. I was for ever thinking that one day someone would have put their foot down and at last the chance came. She had settled down beside me to do her laundry when she suddenly started to complain about my husband. He was so noisy she couldn't sleep at nights. 'Such a racket he makes . . . I don't know what all that row was about last night . . .' Her whining voice went on and on until I could no longer contain myself. 'This is it' I thought, and began to bring out all the things I had been storing up inside me for so long.

'Look, you and me, we're just the same, we're both tenants here. I haven't said anything before but if you're so unhappy with us, you only have to move somewhere else; if I'm unhappy with you, I can move. We're all of us mere tenants, so how come you're always complaining? You're busy all day and keep the light lit till late at night? It's the same for us. I get home late and I never get to sleep till after twelve; you starting to grumble at four in the morning or going to get water then, it's just as annoying. If you're unhappy with us, you'd better move out, surely?'

I brought it all out without a pause for breath; then I suddenly thought that I ought to include the fight of a few weeks before. Actually, in all my life I had almost never fought with anyone, but I had made up my mind that if I was going to fight I would do it as well as anyone.

'Look, you say your husband's an angel; well so is mine. I never mentioned it before, but really, who ever heard of a burning briquette being thrown into someone's room? What kind of behavior is that towards someone? What's so wrong about telling people to save water or electricity? What was there to make such a fuss over? As for throwing that into our room, who else in this house would do that kind of thing? Anyone would think this house belonged to you. Since you only rent one room, what gives you the right to raise your voice like that? If you want to report us for disturbing your rest, go ahead, do it! There's no one to match you when it comes to denouncing other people. The people in the next room come in drunk sometimes; how come you're always shouting out that you'll report them? Go ahead, do it, I say, do it!'

All the resentment I had kept bottled up from the time of the briquette incident suddenly came bursting out, and my voice rose higher and higher as I berated Kyongae's mother. To illustrate my determination never again to tolerate such behavior, I threw open the door of our room and made a solemn promise to my husband.

'From now on, swear at this woman as much as you like. I'll stand up for you.'

'I told you before. She was the one who started it.'

'In future, if you want to swear at her, go right ahead and do it. Swear all you like; she only looks like a human being.'

That was the end of the fight. Perhaps she was dumbfounded on seeing me so totally unlike my ordinary self; anyway, she answered me not a single word. For over a week no words passed between us. It was rather quiet; then one day she casually spoke and we were reconciled. After that one scene we never fought again. If you think about it, poverty was the real culprit. Living together in cramped quarters, things often get on your nerves.

After spending five years in that shack, we moved into our final home. My brother's lungs had always been bad; he lived in this house with our mother while his wife kept a shop down in Seoul, where she lived with their children. Early in 1985 he died. Mother had the kitchen made into an extra room and asked us to come and live with her.

The two rooms were side by side; my husband had the smaller room to himself while mother and I used the slightly larger one. The little door between the two rooms was always kept open, it was like a single room. At first I shared the room with him but it was so small it took only one person lying down to fill it and he liked to sleep with the light on, so I moved into mother's room.

Still, since I had to investigate if he started to rummage around in the night or early in the morning, we lived with the door open. All our married life we were on the move from one room to another on the outskirts of Seoul.

Whenever I read this poem about the first house we lived in after we were married, I find myself smiling bitterly:

Our house is thatched, next door's is thatched too.
Our house belongs to the people of Seoul
I've never had dealings with the folk next door.

Three families live in our house, the owner's too,
our population density's at international levels.
Fourteen people in all, no less.

Our house sold off its only dog:
are we a developing country like the papers say?
Next door they've put up a TV antenna
they're really advanced.

(From: 'At the foot of Mount Surak')

In those days he used to say that with fourteen people crammed under a single roof, we were at international levels for density of population. Only later things got even worse. We found ourselves obliged to squeeze into houses where several dozen people were living, and put up with places where the density of population might be less but which were not fit for people to live in at all. Yet everything was always good for him. The view was good, the air good, the people good, everything was 'just fine.'

Especially in the days when we were living at the foot of Mount Surak, he would often go climbing and wrote any number of poems there. 'If you want to go downtown from here by bus, this being the suburbs, it takes about an hour,' he wrote in a poem, 'Suburbs,' composed at this time, and he was all the time saying how good it was there. The water was good, the hills were good, the people kind-hearted, he reckoned it was a 'good place to live.'

'A country bumpkin's a happy man,' he says in a poem, 'Country bumpkin,' written after we had moved to the outskirts of Ŭijŏngbu. I find it hard to decide if he really meant it when he said such things, or if he was only saying them; but looking back now, I can say that those years we spent moving from one rented room to another were really beautiful. We were sometimes so poor that our only meal for the day was a single block of dried noodles boiled up and shared, but he was there beside me, alive and breathing.

Always on the move

# Talking with God

I may have been closer to him than anybody else, still the being he felt closest to was God. He used to say, 'God is always with me.' He would describe how God scrutinized his every gesture, step, movement, even read his mind, and punished his every mistake. Since God was so close, he could be found everywhere at every moment. During his waking hours he would all the time be calling on God, talking to him in familiar terms all on his own.

'God, thank you for that tasty food.'

'God, help me write.'

'God, I won't do that again. Forgive me this time.'

I feel sure that if God had not been there for him, he would have collapsed like a tree without roots. It was God who enabled him to order and control his thoughts and deeds in everyday life with his great power, but above all else God was the ground of his very being.

If God had not been there, he would have been nothing but a hollow shell. He would all the time repeat, almost automatically, that he had left the place where God lived for a short outing down here on earth and that soon he would be going back to God; he even bequeathed us the poem 'Back to Heaven' as if he was intent on leaving behind a written testimony to that belief: 'I'll go back to heaven again . . .'

Although he conversed with God all the time, he almost never went to church. He had a Catholic baptismal name, Simon, but he never went to Mass. If an acquaintance urged him to go to church, he would be offended and reply, 'Why bother? God's with me all the time, even if I don't go to church . . .'

From 1982 onward, for rather more than three years, he did regularly attend a protestant church in downtown Seoul, uniquely because he enjoyed the sermons of the pastor there.

Arriving at the church, he would race up the stairs and take his place in the third floor gallery from where he had a clear view of everything below. During the service, if he was moved by the pastor's sermon or the hymn-singing, he would weep copiously. Once the service was over, he was off down the stairs like a shot, shook the pastor's hand exclaiming, 'Pastor, pastor!,' and left. On those occasions when Pastor Kim was abroad and someone else was due to preach, he made no attempt to attend the service.

Once, when a young preacher urged him to attend church regularly, the reply was a curt refusal. On being asked the reason, he explained that he had attained total enlightenment. He was not making a bad joke; simply, once he had expressed a sincere refusal, no preacher or minister had any right to bother him further. He felt that since they had the same God, protestants and catholics ought to unite; he reckoned all the fuss about which one was right was all nonsense. His opinion never varied:

'Do you believe in God? It's so comforting once you believe in God. You should believe in God.'

He wrote a poem called 'Happiness' where he explained how, since God, 'the mightiest person in the whole wide world,' was looking after his interests, he had nothing to worry about.

As a result he used to boast like a child that he was sure to go to heaven. He would never yield an inch, even when everyone laughed at him.

'So all I need to do is hang on to you and I'll go to heaven too?'

'Of course; there's no question of going to hell. God has decided I'm going to heaven. Once we're there we can live without anything at all; it'll be alright.'

If he ever started to talk about heaven, other topics were sure to emerge. He used to enjoy affirming things like: not every minister will go to heaven; God doesn't like going to big churches; it's very painful for the rich to pass through a needle's eye, so it's bad to get rich.

He used to affirm that he knew exactly when he was due to go to heaven. Especially at times when he was unwell, he would tell how God had revealed that he was going to go back to heaven when he was eighty-eight.

He remembered that it had happened at midday one day in April 1982. He was walking along the street in Insa-dong, on his way to the Writers' Association offices, when he suddenly felt tired. He had taken the bus but had dozed off, missed his stop, and had got off at the next.

Those were times when he was drinking *makkoli* instead of eating a proper meal; as a result he was in such a weak state that even having to walk back one bus-stop was a big effort for him and he finally subsided in the shade of a roadside tree. He may have dozed for a while in the pale spring sunlight, he was certainly a bit hazy:

'Don't daydream; just keep on living till you're eighty-eight!'

He stared around, trying to see who had spoken, but there was nobody about. He was convinced that it was the voice of God, telling him that this was not the time for him to die, that he had to go on until he was eighty-eight. So even when he was very ill, he would always insist, 'God is going to keep me alive until I'm eighty-eight,' quite firmly believing that he would not die before.

In the end his belief proved to be wrong, but somehow it gave us all strength. Even when he was sick, I wanted to hold on to that conviction that at least one part of me believed in, and it would give my heart new strength.

So I suppose belief must be a good thing. Some people may think it's all an illusion, but it certainly gives peace to the person who believes.

He was quite sure that he would live to be eighty-eight, right up to his very last breath. In the end he suddenly collapsed and died in the middle of breakfast, without any pain and with no time to experience any fear of death. He didn't make eighty-eight but still I thank God for having taken him peacefully like that.

He always trusted in God for everything, yet he was

afraid of him too, just as much. He used to comment on how dreadful a being he must be to have allowed his only son to be nailed to a cross and suffer like that.

'God, please forgive me.'

All day every day he was all the time repeating those words. God might know what was needed and give everything, he was dreadful too, and sent punishments for misbehavior. That meant that if you realized you had done something wrong, you had to pray and receive forgiveness.

There were a number of things for which he would pray for forgiveness, the most frequent being in connection with drinking. Normally he would abide by the limit he had set himself and not try to drink more than that. If he happened to drink one glass more than usual, he would turn the glass upside down when it was empty and say, 'That's enough,' to mark an end.

Sometimes, though, the desire for a drink refused to go away. On those occasions, the more he longed to drink the more his anxiety grew: 'God's going to send a punishment.' If I was there beside him urging him on, he would be all the more anxious.

'If you keep on drinking, God's sure to punish you.'

'Is that right? Is that right? Will he punish me?'

'You must ask God to forgive you.'

'God, please forgive me, please forgive me; I won't do it again.'

He was convinced that the cirrhosis he was suffering from was a punishment from God. Therefore no matter how intense his craving for a drink, I had only to remind him of his cirrhosis to provoke an instant reaction. Occasionally he could not get to sleep and longed for a glass of beer. At those times we would quarrel.

'I can't get to sleep, can't get to sleep . . . Isn't there something that will help? I feel like a beer!'

'Don't you know what time it is? It's past midnight. There isn't any beer. Drink some fruit juice.'

'Ok, juice will do!'

A moment would pass.

'Oh dear, I do feel like just one glass of beer.'

'You're going to make me angry.'

'Alright, let's sleep. You must go to bed, *Mundi Kashina.*'

'It's because of too much drinking that you're sick; if you keep on like that God is surely going to punish you. You said it was a punishment, didn't you? Your cirrhosis?'

'Oh dear, alright. Now I pray that my angel will help me sleep well, please.'

He always prayed God to forgive him the very second he realized he'd done something wrong; sometimes he would even pray for mistakes I had made instead. There are times when my face betrays my real feelings, when I am tired or not well. It only took him one look to see when I was in a bad mood, then he would lecture me: 'You ought to keep smiling, come what may; don't look so glum. God will punish you.' I would quickly correct my expression. 'That's the way, that's the way!' he would rejoice.

If I remained angry or peevish for too long, he would scold me.

'*Mundi Kashina,* with all those sins you'll not get to heaven.'

'Ok, I'll go to hell with all my sins, you go on up to heaven alone. If I go to hell I'll most likely meet lots more people, what's the point of going to heaven? You go on your own.'

'*SSangnyŏngŭi Kashina,* don't you realize how good it is in heaven and how awful it is in hell? Forgive her, God, please. How could I live if I went to heaven on my own? Please forgive her.'

I would sometimes provoke him, just to see how he would react. If I asked what on earth was the point of reading the Bible, he would scold me in tones of deep disappointment.

'There are no lies in the Bible, you say? Of course there are lies.'

'Not at all! You're just plain ignorant. Why, you haven't even read the Bible . . .'

'That's right, I'm ignorant. I'm ignorant, so I don't read the Bible. Yet you still say that if I hold on tight to you I'll get to heaven.'

'Lord God, forgive her, she's ignorant; forgive her, God.'

He turned to God anxiously, just like children ought to do. Once he composed some Notes on his poetry:

> Faith is a matter of believing in an Absolute Being. How can we live if we do not know what the essence of this world is? Since there is this Absolute Being, how can we live without knowing him?

> Belief is the main principle in my life. How could I ever write poems without that fundamental principle? Speaking for myself, without that principle, I would be far too helpless a being.

Thanks to God, he could enjoy life in this world, and thanks to God he could dream of the world to come. I see those lines as being his confession of faith. Faith was his mainstay in life.

'God, forgive me, please,' was no mindless repetition of words, it was his way of stilling his heart and the prayer by which he asked for redemption by the forgiveness of sins. Once he had purified his heart by that prayer, which was a kind of invocation, he was able to write poems with a blissful heart.

He may have looked like a lapsed, careless Catholic, never going to Mass, and just repeating 'God, forgive me, please,' like a little child, I am convinced that those words were his *Agnus Dei.* It may be a foolish thing to say but I firmly believe that the poet alive and breathing in so many readers' hearts is God's dearly beloved son Simon.

# Poems, beer, and cucumbers

'This is my little sister. Now, say hello, my dear. This is Ch'ŏn Sang-pyŏng . . .'

As my brother presented him I ducked my head in greeting, before taking a seat and taking a second look.

That poet, Ch'ŏn Sang-pyŏng, stood out from the rest in a special way. The longer I stayed, the odder I felt he was. He was nothing at all to look at, and his actions were funny too. He sat picking at his nose until something funny was said, when he would make the tea-room rafters ring with a loud crowing laugh; there was nothing about him that a teenage schoolgirl could find attractive.

Such was our first encounter, thirty-eight years ago, in one corner of the Kalch'ei tea-room in downtown Seoul's Myŏng-dong district. In those days I was a second grade pupil in the girls' high school down in the rural town of Sangju. During the summer holidays I had come up to spend some time with my older brother, who was editor of a weekly paper known as 'The Education Weekly' and he had brought me with him to say hello to some of his literary friends.

In those years, an artist was an artist, an aspiring artist was an aspirant, but all without exception haunted the alleys of Myŏng-dong. They each had their favorite hideouts, with names like Kalch'ei, Tolch'ei, Renaissance, Ŭnsŏng . . . . Writers, musicians, artists would congregate there, discussing aesthetics, putting together reviews, radiating all the fervor of youth.

The tea-rooms and bars of those days were nothing like today's. Certainly, they earned a living by selling tea and drinks to artists, but in return they served as the artists' offices and sometimes even supported them financially. They were places full of romance and of real human kindness.

I was no artist, not even an aspiring one, but I spent much of my youth there. I was no writer, but I came to consider many writers as an older or younger brother, as my friends. If I was able to experience my 'Myŏng-dong period' like them, it was thanks to my brother's having brought me there as he did.

Anyway, that is how Ch'ŏn Sang-pyŏng and I knotted the first thread of our common destiny and from that moment on we unreservedly treated one another as older brother and younger sister.

On further enquiry, Ch'ŏn Sang-pyŏng turned out to be a well-known poet and critic, a young man of whom much was expected in the future. My brother was all the time repeating, 'That Sang-pyŏng's a real genius, he really is,' praising him to the skies, and if he came into any money he would pay off what he owed for drinks at the Ŭnsŏng.

The reason why the river flows toward the sea
is not only because I've been weeping
all day long
up on the hill.

Not only because I've been blooming
like a sunflower in longing
all night long
up on the hill.

The reason I've been weeping like a beast in sorrow
up on the hill
is not only because
the river flows toward the sea.

That is the poem 'River Waters' by which he was first introduced to the literary world. The story is now a well-known one. He was still only in the fifth grade of Masan Middle School when it was published in the review *Munye,* on the recommendation of the poet Yu Ch'i-hwan.

He used to tell how, one Harvest Moon Festival, he had gone up the hill behind his home and was looking out to sea when the sight of people weeping as they paid their respects at the family tombs brought the poem to his mind. It was a poem expressing the transience of human existence that had come home to him in the thought, 'Why, everyone is bound to die.'

His form-master in those days was Kim Ch'un-su, who was later to become one of Korea's senior poets. It was the strong emotion he experienced on reading his volume entitled 'Clouds and Roses' that first made him decide that he too would write poems.

Not long after he had shown the poem 'River Waters' to his teacher, a class-mate casually remarked, 'I saw something in a book by someone with just the same name as you.' A visit to the bookstore established that 'River Waters' had been published, with his name attached; he was officially launched. In addition, he was later recognized as a critic and at the time when I first met him he was busily engaged in writing critical essays.

Any number of people kept after him to write a review for them but even in the case of a friend, if he did not like the work he would refuse and swear: 'You scoundrel! Did you write this or steal it? You think calling something a work of literature is reason enough for publishing it?'

To the very end of his life, he never changed in that respect. If he was sent newly published volumes of poetry he would read them, then write a review. He particularly detested poets who wrote in a difficult style.

'What the hell is he talking about? Does the idiot call this poetry? Poetry has to be written so that people can feel it easily and get the meaning. Just take a look at this, I ask you, what the hell is he on about?'

Then he would slam the desk shut or throw the book aside.

On the other hand, if ever a poem pleased him, he was delighted.

'Isn't this great? It's better than anything I could write.

Isn't it great?' He would invite me to share his opinion.

'Poetry must never be difficult.'

He always said the same thing, right to the end. He himself used easy words when he wrote poetry. Sometimes I would ask him, 'Isn't it too simple if you write like that?' to which he would merely reply, 'It's a poem based on life.'

He used to say that 'belief' and 'life' were the basis of poetry. If you were too lonely you couldn't write poetry, obedience to God's Word meant not being lonely, you had to be happy. He also said that if you loved life, you could feel something in even life's humblest events and write poems on that.

> Life is vast. Even when you are quietly sitting alone, there's poetry. You need only shut your eyes and poetry invariably goes rolling by. You only have to grab hold of it for a poem to be born . . .

> I face life with pure eyes. Therefore I find poetry in humble things. That is why life is my poetry.

As he explained in his Notes, he really loved poems based on life. My mother and niece, the two puppies, our whole family became the subject of poems where the words he used were simple, like ordinary speech.

That does not mean that he wrote without any thought. If an idea struck him or if he received a request for a poem, he would take his time, spending ages sitting alone, composing and deleting, composing and deleting mentally. Then once he took up his pen, he would dash off the whole poem without pausing or correcting anything. He never lost his conviction that writing a poem was the important thing, and that the form in which it was written did not matter. His notepaper might not be clean, but spotted and stained with drops of beer, still he wrote, with a pencil or a ballpoint pen, whatever came to hand.

If some beer got spilt so that the writing was smeared and illegible, he would make no attempt to correct it. There was no point in protesting, either.

'What's this? Write it again.'

'I won't. You copy it out or else give it as it is, I'm not going to look at it again. I don't want to know!'

Once he had finished, it was done with. Once he had written, he never revised anything.

He never wrote critical essays about his own poetry. If I read something he had written, he would ask, 'Is it ok? Is it ok?' That was all.

Sometimes he would torment himself about the title: 'What shall we call it? What title?' and I would express my own ideas. If something I said pleased him he would be unstinting in his praise. 'Oh, that's very good. How do you know so much?'

He had no regular rhythm in writing. Sometimes the deadline for a commission arrived and he had to rush, sometimes he had plenty of time but an idea came to him and he would write on the spot. If he happened to feel bored and phoned me at Kwich'ŏn I would urge him to write a poem. He would reply 'Ok,' hang up, then call me an hour later: 'I've written a poem.'

On days when he wrote a poem, he would place the manuscript by his pillow and lie there with his eyes shut tight. When I got home, I would read the poem first, before eating my supper. Only then, when I said, 'I'm home,' would he show any sign of realizing I was home.

'You're home, you're home. I wrote a poem and put it there. Did you see it? Is it alright?'

Even if I told him to change something, he never would; yet he invariably asked me what I thought.

He was really proud of being a poet. He used to say that poetry was the king of literature and the poet the highest kind of writer. A poem, he would say, is always written truthfully, following the promptings of the heart, according to one's inner feelings, while anyone who wants to write a novel has to tell lies; therefore poetry comes first.

Not that he was necessarily talking of himself when he said that 'the poet is the highest' but still, when you heard him say, 'I'm a poet, ever so many people know me,' it was easy to sense an element of pride. Of all our poets, he used to revere Sŏ Chŏng-ju as 'the most poetic of poets' and he was enormously fond of his lyrics.

One of his poems has the mysterious title *So Nung Jo* (which means 'Song of a small tomb'). I remember him explaining that he wanted to become as great a poet as the classical Chinese poet Tu Fu and that therefore he had given the poem that poet's pen-name as its title. The poem left a deep impression on me because it marks the first and last time that he ever dreamed of writing 'like somebody.' It was written to mark *Chusŏk* (the autumn festival) of 1970:

Father and mother lie
in the family burial plot at home

I'm all on my own
here in Seoul

brother and sisters
are down in Pusan

I don't have the fare
so I can't go.

If there's a fare to pay
when you pass away

does that mean
I'll never be able to go?

When you think of it, ah,
what a deep thing life is.

I cannot believe that it really matters very much whether he became as great a poet as Tu Fu or not. As he strove to write his poems he knew happiness and gratitude. Surely that is enough.

'I am happy, even though I am poor and sad. It is as a result of my happiness that this book of poems has come to birth.'

Once I read something he had written to that effect in his Notes on his poems, and realized that my conjecture was right. Yet in order to be able to write poems in a happy frame of mind, there was something he more or less had to have: beer and cucumbers. When inspiration would not come, or when a poem was poised unwilling to emerge, I only had to serve that and it was better than any magic spell in producing a poem quite painlessly. Poetry, beer, and cucumbers were a trinity that belonged together all his life.

He loved cucumbers. To such a point that he would sometimes ring Kwich'ŏn: 'Be sure to bring some cucumbers,' or complain: 'There are no cucumbers, I can't eat anything.'

If we served him beer and cucumbers, he would soon grow happy and say that he could feel a poem trying to come out. If ever mother gave him some small cucumbers and a glass of beer he would be sure to phone me.

'Guess what! Ma's just brought me some cucumbers and a glass of beer to drink; I feel so good. I'm sure a poem's coming. Thanks dear, thank you.'

If he needed to write a poem and got writer's block, he would consider cucumbers as a kind of medicine.

'It's because I've not got any cucumbers that I can't write. Tell *Ŏmma* to get another bottle of beer. I just can't write any poetry at all.'

'Alright. I'll bring some home with me.'

He claimed he needed cucumbers whenever he wrote a poem, yet he composed his most popular lyric '*Kwich'ŏn*' (Back to Heaven) as well as his first recognized poem 'River Waters' without their help. Were those cucumbers really a way of preparing to write poetry? Or were they a witty ploy to get an extra drink of beer? I don't know. One thing is sure: when there were cucumbers, he was happy, and a poem would come to birth.

# Our children

'It would have been nice to have had children, a boy or a girl . . . very nice . . . When I went to the Korea Central Intelligence Agency that time, if they'd given me electric shock torture just twice, I could still have had kids, it was the third time that did it. Those bastards.'

He was like a child, and sometimes he used to intone a lament for our lack of children. He was so intensely fond of them; sometimes he must have felt very sad at not having any of his own.

He used to say that children were the creatures closest to God in innocence and that it was because of that innocence that he loved them. There might not be children in our house, we had at least as many pictures of children as any other family, precisely on account of his extraordinary love of children. Whenever the photo of a child appeared in a newspaper, a magazine, a calendar, anywhere, he would cut it out. At one time it seemed he would paper the whole room with them.

He also received photos of the children of people he knew; he would put them on his desk or on the wall, then speak to them when he had nothing else to do: '*Yonom*

*Yonom Yo Yeppŭn Nom* You fine fellow, you fine fellow, you lovely fellow, you.'

He was just like a child himself, and he kept repeating, 'So pretty, so cute,' while he gazed lovingly at the children in the pictures,

The photo of Bok-nam was one he was specially fond of. It was the face of a child, photographed somewhere by a professional photographer; he gave it the name Bok-nam himself. He used to hold conversations with it, on his own, calling out, 'Bok-nama, Bok-nama.' Having those talks with Bok-nam really used to cheer him up.

He was so fond of children that even when he was seriously ill himself, the sight of a child going past was enough to make him forget completely his own situation.

Five years before he died, at the moment when he had just been diagnosed as having acute cirrhosis, we were agonizing as to whether or not he should be admitted to a big hospital. Suddenly a child went past, clutching its mother's hand, and he burst out, '*Yonom Yonom Yonom,*' as if he wanted to go running after it, he felt so fond of children.

Seeing him there, holding his great stomach all swollen like a balloon, yet so happy to see a child that he seemed for a moment to have forgotten he was sick, I felt overwhelmed with admiration and at the same time so utterly sad that I began to cry.

He was so fond of children that all the children he came across became his friends. He made friends with the children living around our house, and with the children that came to Kwich'ŏn.

Whenever a child called him '*Haraboji* Grand-dad!' he would be so delighted he would always respond '*Yonom! Yonom*!' which is why the local children at home gave him the nickname '*Yonom haraboji*.' Their *Yonom haraboji* would sometimes go out with a hundred Won coin, spend it on biscuits for them, and come in after playing with them for a time.

'What did you spend all your money on?'

'On my friends.'

'What friends? Come on, speak up.'

'I've got friends. Friends you don't know.'

He never told me but you only had to see his happy expression to know. He'd been out playing marbles with angels from heaven.

It's really very fortunate, given his love of children, that he had creatures around him as loveable as children would have been. Our children were Bokshil --'just like my son'-- and my 'daughter' Tolltoll. Tolltoll was the eight-year old mother of Bokshil, while he was still only a puppy of less than two, and we treated those two dogs just like people, giving and receiving intense affection.

People often say that 'animals are just the same as humans,' and we were able to verify the truth of it in bringing up our dogs. We saw it when we marked the forty-ninth day after his death. After visiting the grave, the group of friends came and spent a moment down at the house. They were gazing silently into the now owner-less room when my mother, seized with a fit of grief, began to cry. Immediately Tolltoll, who was sitting beside her, started to cry too. Seeing her mournful eyes, that showed she understood everything that was happening even without words, I sensed strongly that she really was just like a human being.

Tolltoll is one of the dogs
we keep at home.

There's another, Bokshil,
just one year old;
Tolltoll's his mother.

I have never once heard
Tolltoll barking.

She's so gentle and well-mannered.
Truly a dog of silence.

She treats everyone equally
so if a thief comes in
I'm worried what will happen.

That is just one of the unpublished poems he wrote about our puppies.

'Bokshil is mine; he's just like my son. Tolltoll's your daughter!'

As a result of those words, our dogs got themselves family names. Yŏng-jin once having called Bokshil 'Ch'ŏn Bokshil' it was only natural that Tolltoll should come to be known by my name as 'Mok Tolltoll.'

Tolltoll was Bokshil's mother. There were five in the litter but from the day they were born, he was especially beautiful. They were only mongrels, but with his soft white fur and jet-black eyes under their creased lids, he was truly cute.

My husband paid no attention to the other puppies but unashamedly began to treat Bokshil like a child. Not only would they lie back to back with their heads on the same pillow, but at mealtimes he would always be sure to give Bokshil a piece of his meat.

As if aware of how fond he was of him, whenever my husband went out somewhere, Bokshil would go into his room and refuse to leave it. No matter how sternly my mother ordered him out, he would ignore her and stay there for one hour, two hours. He paid no attention to us or to neighbors, but if a stranger came in he would station himself at the entrance to the room and lie there, firmly refusing to let them in until my husband came back.

Bokshil later began to torment us all, especially my husband. When he was about fifteen months old, he began to have an affair. It was summer, on the first of the three days when many people like to eat dog meat. Suddenly Bokshil was gone. We were specially worried, seeing what day it was, in case he had been carried off by a dog-seller. The neighbors all turned out and searched, but there was no sign of him.

Two days later he came trotting in.

'You little wretch! Where have you been off to?'

Grabbing hold of him, my husband was speechless for joy.

Ten days or so later, on the second dog-meat day, Bokshil vanished again. This time there was not a trace of him for four whole days. Ma went climbing the nearby hills calling for him, all the neighbors went out in search parties.

'He was so pretty, some passers-by must have taken him.'

'Suppose it was a dog-merchant?'

Opinions were divided. Supposing someone had carried him off, it would be alright so long as they treated him well; but if it was a dog-seller, how terrible. In those days there was a place just behind our house where some people raised dogs for meat, which meant that dog-merchants often came around. It is wrong to suspect anyone without due cause, but the situation lent itself to ominous speculations.

Four days had passed when Bokshil once again came trotting in of his own accord. Anticipating that Ma would scold him, the cunning Bokshil dashed into the room and played cute. He was so winsome that no one could ever scold him, even when he deserved it.

Bokshil's sweetheart lived in a butcher's house a long way away from our neighborhood. Ten days later he was off again, and so it continued. I explained to my husband what was happening.

'He's having an affair. He's off after a woman.'

'You naughty wretch, are you having an affair? You wretch, you've found another home, have you? And you ask them to feed you too!'

'If you scold him too much, suppose he goes there

and won't come back?'

'You think he would?'

From that moment, he only cursed him inwardly: 'Thieving pup, wretched pup.' Having had his fling, Bokshil duly became the father of a litter of four pups. I saw with my own eyes that one of them was the spitting image of Bokshil.

Bokshil too had by now reached a respectable age but in our eyes both dogs remained like children. I would always feed them before I had breakfast in the morning, and see to them before eating my own supper in the evening too. They would always refuse to eat unless I gave them their food, going without, even if it was midnight by the time I got home. There was no point in Ma trying to feed them; she admired the fact and deplored it at the same time.

'First there's that one big baby, and the animals are just the same. Why do they have to give you so much trouble?'

Perhaps because he was so young, I always had to stroke Bokshil when I gave him his food. Tolltoll would eat on her own but she was jealous. So I had to feed and stroke first one, then the other. Otherwise Tolltoll would be hurt and start to cry.

When that happened I was obliged to comfort her: 'Why, Tolltoll, you're the prettiest. You're the prettiest one in the world.'

Just as we know what people are feeling by their eyes, animals like it if you look them straight in the eye. I was obliged to give both animals exactly the same degree of fuss. It was just like parents who hurt their children by showing favoritism.

When we got up in the morning and opened the door onto the garden, Tolltoll and Bokshil would invariably dash in as if to show they'd been waiting, butting us affectionately with their heads. It was their way of wishing us good morning.

Every evening they were sure to come out to the bus-stop to meet me. They were so impatient that Ma could never fail to come to meet me. If ever she forgot the time, they would scold her, running up and down and yelping.

As a result, every time I got off the little bus I found what looked like a photo waiting for me. Ma would be sitting down, with Bokshil squatting at her feet and Tolltoll reclining. Except when Bokshil was off roaming, nothing ever changed in that harmonious family group.

My husband liked eggs, there always had to be a dish of scrambled eggs on his breakfast table. Tolltoll and Bokshil seemed to take after him, they were fond of eggs too. They had a remarkable knack, if you gave them an egg, of striking it with their paw until it broke and they could eat it. The egg-seller agreed to give them any broken eggs he had when he passed. The wretches soon learned this, and would go rushing out to the egg van at the first sound of 'Eggs for sale!' on the loudspeaker, dancing around in expectation.

If anyone says, 'Let's take a picture,' they duly strike a pose. If you scold them with, 'How dare you come into the room with dirty feet?' they rush out, wipe them, then return. All that has changed is that the master, who used to be so eagerly on the lookout for them when he came back from anywhere, is no longer to be seen.

Yet he may well be enjoying himself more than ever. Since he has undoubtedly 'gone back to Heaven,' he may well be playing marbles, not now with 'angels from heaven' but with real angels up in heaven.

Our children

# Love and Kwich'ŏn

I sometimes find myself wondering: take away the label 'wife of Ch'ŏn Sang-pyŏng the poet' and what would remain of me? Women who have spent their whole lives as their husbands' shadows often find themselves trying to evaluate their own personal lives in this way later on. For my husband, poetry and God were the reward and central values of his life; so what 'treasure' do I have?

Now that I no longer have a husband beside me, the reply has become clearer. What remains is the little business I set up as devotedly as the affection I felt for him. Kwich'ŏn may be nothing but a tiny Korean tea-room, for me it is a supremely precious space.

Above all, Kwich'ŏn became the foundation of our married life, since it enabled us to solve the problem of earning a living, after years when we were often hungry. It was also the place where, apart from our home, I spent most hours with my husband and it became the spot where we were able to share moments of love with many people who cared for us both.

Kwich'ŏn first opened in March 1985. In all the time

since then, there has not been a single day when the door has stayed shut. The reason why it has been open every day with never a day off, 365 days a year for all these years, until today, why there always has to be someone in attendance, is because I cannot stand the thought of even a single customer arriving and being obliged to leave again because the door was shut.

On public holidays I felt I had to open because it was a holiday. There are people who for various reasons are ill at ease staying home. I had the feeling that it would be very fortunate for them at such times if there was somewhere they could get out and go to for a rest and a cup of tea.

As a result, the notion that 'Kwich'ŏn is always open' became firmly established in people's minds and because it was unthinkable that I should disappoint customers who came with that idea, I duly opened.

Even if I feel tired or am busy with other things, I have always made a point of being there on time. My customers give me no leisure to be lazy, because if they find I'm not there they leave again: 'Isn't she here? I'll come back a bit later.' If the young friends I leave in charge say that I've gone out for my lunch, they don't order their tea until I come back.

It's just the same tea, yet if someone else makes it I hear them say, 'It's tasteless,' 'It tastes a bit different,' and I know that they don't come to Kwich'ŏn for the taste of the tea but for human warmth. I keep feeling it.

If Kwich'ŏn got started, it was entirely thanks to the help of people around us. The poet Kang Tae-Yŏl, an old friend of my brother's and my husband's, learning what a hard time we were having, suggested opening some kind of business. I still remember clearly what he said as he casually offered to lend me three million Won.

'I'll be happy if it means you can buy our Ch'on his *makkŏli,* at least. You can pay me back whenever you're in a position to, and don't go worrying yourself about things like interest . . .'

Fortified by that kind exhortation, I resolved to open Kwich'ŏn. I paid a deposit of two and a half million for the room; then, needing more money, I borrowed one million from a money-lender on daily interest. With that I bought chairs and tables, some straw lamp-shades, and so on, repaired the room a bit, and did my best to create the right atmosphere for a tea-room. I covered the lamp-shades with swathes of colored paper; arranged a few books on the shelves set in one of the walls; I bought roughly made pottery cups that would best bring out the perfume of the quince and citron tea. . .

My purse was empty, I was exhausted, but I had set out to prepare something for the future, and my heart was swollen with happiness. It was a small room, with just four or five little tables, space for a maximum of twenty people at a pinch; I called it 'Kwich'ŏn' after my husband's most famous poem.

So I began my business, selling citron tea and quince tea, with cold rice punch and cinnamon tea in the summer as well, with exhibitions of small paintings and wooden sculptures that I sometimes sold.

At first, charging seven hundred Won per cup, I

could just about break even with thirty customers a day. Out of the day's income of some twenty thousand Won, twelve thousand went to repay the money-lender; the remaining nine thousand had to cover the cost of the various materials and our daily living expenses. I repaid the initial loan of one million in about a hundred days and since then I've continued to borrow and repay as necessary.

I never used to have a penny I could call my own but nowadays, with the money I borrow, I sometimes buy small paintings by artists living in the neighborhood who are having a hard time. They often spontaneously make a special price for me. There are some who, when they need money, ask me directly: '*Samonim*, buy a painting, won't you?.' There are others who can't bring themselves to say anything. When the holiday seasons come, I give one or two hundred thousand Won to friends like that whom I feel a special concern for. Then, circumstances permitting, they sometimes bring me one of their paintings in return and suggest I sell it.

Even though I still borrow when I have to, the fact of being able to buy paintings and carvings, and still have a thousand Won or ten thousand Won to put into a savings account, gives me the impression I have become very rich.

When I recall the days when we had to go without meals, and walk miles because there was no money for the bus fare, I am reminded of the old proverb: No matter how hard things get, life still goes on, for everyone. I live with a strong feeling that if I have received from others there also comes a time when I can give to others.

When Kwich'ŏn first opened there were plenty of customers who came out of curiosity, because they had heard that 'What's-her-name the wife of the poet Ch'ŏn Sang-pyŏng' was running it. Although it was called a tea-room, there were those who stubbornly demanded *makkŏlli,* asking in amazement why I didn't sell liquor when Ch'ŏn Sang-pyŏng was so fond of a drink. There were quite a few who came less thinking of the tea than eager to see the couple running it.

In addition, perhaps aware of my husband's reputation for eccentricity, all the oddballs in the country came thronging in. There were all kinds of eccentrics, and there were some customers who merely pretended to be odd. There were those who tried to attract attention by the oddity of their clothes, or their speech, or their actions. Such people, having played the eccentric once or twice and realizing that I did not approve, generally reverted to being well-behaved customers.

Once two men came in, presenting themselves as 'taffy-sellers from Chŏlla.' Their clothes were soaked with the early springtime rain but in they came, carrying armfuls of forsythia they claimed to have picked somewhere out Kimpo way. I don't know if they wanted to be taken for bohemian eccentrics, but anyway they immediately began to address the customers in coarse terms, making a regular nuisance of themselves.

'We've come up from Chŏlla to work as taffy-sellers. And who are you then, eh?'

At first, as they noisily clacked the scissors they carried and put on odd expressions, everyone just laughed;

but at length they went too far and the smiles turned into frowns.

'Look, you say you've come here for the sake of Ch'ŏn Sang-pyŏng, yet if you keep on bothering the customers like this, how can I do any business?'

'*Samonim*, we're sorry. We didn't mean any harm.'

'For goodness sake, sit down.'

'We don't have any money; will you still serve us?'

'I can give you the tea.'

They replied meekly, proffered deep bows, and sat down, apparently getting themselves under control.

They drank their tea and left; some time later they came back. They looked as if they had been drinking. This time driven by drunkenness, they once again began to annoy the other customers.

'*Samonim*, we've brought money this time, so give us a cup of tea, will you?'

'I don't care if you've got money, I'm not selling you any tea. You can't behave like this. I'll let you have tea if you come tomorrow, but not today. Be off with you, quickly.'

'I don't want to. I'm not going.'

'What? Are you really not going? Do I have to start shouting and shame you into going? Be off, quickly. Today, it's because you've been drinking; let's see how it goes tomorrow.'

'Since you say so, we'll go.'

Those two had stayed firmly sitting when some of the younger customers attempted to force them out, and had continued to sit there even when people tried to coax them out; but as soon as I got really angry, off they went. Outside the door there was another rumpus while they dropped to their knees in a deep prostration, then things quietened down.

The next day one of them came by on his own, pulling a cart. He was on the verge of tears because Seoul people were so unkind, he wasn't doing any business. I gave him a cup of tea as a way of making up for the day before. Emerging after sitting inside for a while, he found his cart had gone. He went rushing off to the trash collection point in the nearby market, where his cart had been taken by the ward office officials, and he came back with a different cart he had been given by the ward office.

'Did you ever? They ought to be punished for giving people such turns.'

'They ought indeed.'

He reacted remarkably calmly, it seemed to have given him a fright; he still drops in at Kwich'ŏn sometimes. He even came by once saying that his mother had come up from Chŏlla Province, and he'd bought two mackerel for her but he wanted me to have one of them. Irrespectively porter or laborer, energetically earning money, whenever he changed jobs he would come by to find out how I was.

We gave that young man the nickname 'Taffy-seller'; his bright smile has such an innocent air to it. I suppose it's because he has that innocent side to him that he could get away with his behavior so easily.

In any case, real oddballs and oddballs that were not oddballs, apparently flocking in from every corner of the country, thronged Kwich'ŏn in the early days, and it was hard work dealing with them, but at the same time I enjoyed the novelty of meeting so many unusual people.

In contrast to them, there were also a lot of people who deprived themselves of such good encounters because of money.

'*Samonim,* I left my jacket on the bus with my wallet in it. If you could just let me have twenty thousand Won, I'll pay it back into your bank account at once.'

'*Samonim,* it's the New Year holidays, all the banks are shut and I can't get any money. Lend me ten thousand Won.'

'*Samonim,* I was drunk and I broke a window when I fell down; I have to pay for it and I don't have enough. Could you lend me fifteen thousand?'

Inevitably there were customers asking me to lend them money on various pretexts. Since I was making a fair amount each day, I could hardly refuse. I used to think, 'If you pay it back, ok, and if you don't, that's the end of it,' as I lent what they asked for and most often heard nothing more. Nowadays I can usually tell if they're lying or not but I still let myself be duped into giving.

It's not the fact of not getting my money back that I regret, it's the fact of producing people unable to repay. If someone doesn't have the money, they need only make a phone call to say that they can't come by for this or that reason, they'll repay it some other time; what makes me feel upset is people who never appear again on account of ten or twenty thousand Won.

Still, the vast majority of customers visiting Kwich'ŏn are very fond of me and my tea-room, and that makes me feel very proud.

From the day I first opened Kwich'ŏn until now, I have never lost the idea that the people coming are not so much customers coming to drink a cup of tea in a tea-room, as guests visiting my home, guests just like members of my own family.

First of all, the small space naturally makes people feel as if they know each other. They sit down wherever there's room and that's fine. Customers coming for the first time shrink and look embarrassed when a regular customer comes in and plonks himself down next to them, but the regulars gently explain: 'It's a tight squeeze in here, so any vacant seat has to be used.'

The customers sort out seating problems among themselves. They invite others to come and sit down, making room beside them or in front of them. Strangers sitting side by side or opposite one another start to talk and soon become friends. At least three marriages have resulted from chance encounters at Kwich'ŏn, something which makes me very happy.

Perhaps because I have seen so many customers, I can generally guess a person's character at first sight and I remember the particular likings of regular customers.

'Aha,' I guess, 'this one likes it sweet,' 'Um, this one will be happier if it's not too sweet,' and they're all astonished: 'But how did you know that's how I like my tea?'

Sometimes I see students, whose finances are inevitably fragile, stay sitting after they've finished drinking their tea, twirling the teaspoon idly; experience has taught me that it's a sure sign that they are longing for more.

So I ask: 'Would you like another cup?' Invariably they reply, 'Oh yes.' The second cup is on me, in those cases.

When I think, 'It's two thousand Won a cup,' I turn into a business woman who puts money first; but when I decide, 'This one's on me,' I feel like a kindly next-door neighbor, it makes me feel good.

Several years ago, a couple due to go to study in Italy did their conversation practice in Kwich'ŏn. They would start at ten in the morning, three days a week, and in order to be there on time to welcome them I had to leave home earlier than usual. While they were studying, I would serve them two cups of quince tea and two of citron. It was as if that helped them study; they were so enthusiastic, it was a pleasure to see them.

After spending a few months in that way, they left to study abroad and soon after that the girl's parents become regular customers, while a Korean from Japan she had taught would likewise drop in every time he had a guest.

Every letter they sent mentioned my quince tea, so last summer I sent them a coffee jar full of the candied quince slices used to prepare it. They made extravagant promises: 'Once we have succeeded we will repay all your kindnesses,' but they were elated at the way my little gestures of love made me and them feel so good.

I consider the young folk coming to Kwich'ŏn as my sons and daughters, and that means there have been times when this one or that one earned themselves a sharp scolding. Now and then one left a taxi standing outside while they ran in to ask me for money for the fare. I would quietly pay the fare, then scold them till they felt really ashamed.

'If you haven't got the taxi fare, you must walk. What need was there for you to come by taxi?'

Even though I scolded them, they took it laughing. I suppose that's why they say it's good to be young.

There's one rather wild young monk who often comes, who also got his share of scoldings.

'What sort of good-for-nothing monk are you? You'd do better to unfrock yourself and do something worthwhile.'

'*Aigo*, why do you say that? Give over.'

'I'm saying you shouldn't bring shame onto proper monks.'

'*Aigo*, it's all because I drank too much yesterday. I drank till I got really sloshed.'

'Why, how can a monk talk like that? You're not qualified to be a monk.'

Sending him off after giving him a stern telling-off, I didn't feel very happy myself but I reckon he knew that I was scolding him with feelings like those I would have had for a son.

What I want to share with all these people is a heart warm as a cup of hot tea. Yet there are times when they manifest even greater affection towards me.

Sometimes I leave one of them in charge while I go off to have my lunch; where are you going to find a store-keeper as happy as I am? I have these customers who are not customers but come along, serve the tea, do the washing up, and collect the money for me as well.

Now Kwich'ŏn is starting to get on in years, there are more and more customers who come because they like me, apart from any thought of my husband; seeing that, I have the impression that my modest devotion has grown into a tower of love.

There's the friend who heard of my husband's death and flew in from America to hold my hand at the forty-ninth day's ceremony; friends who regularly phone or write with news while they are travelling in the countryside or abroad; friends who wait several hours to be able to drink a cup of tea made by me. . .

Here I stand, surrounded by a great throng of people who are like daughters and sons, friends, elder and younger brothers and sisters to me; how lucky I am, and how happy.

What can be more precious than encounters with people?

*Translator's note*: The original Kwich'ŏn no longer exists. The building was destroyed and the site redeveloped. Mok Sun-ok opened a new café in an alley closer to Anguk-dong a couple of years before. Then late in 2005 she opened a small Kwich'ŏn café in the large building built on the site of the old one.

## Strange ways with money

'You'll go on running Kwich'ŏn till you're seventy! You need to earn seventy million Won, so keep saving!'

He would all the time be telling me that. He meant that by running Kwich'ŏn until I was seventy years old, I would be able to save seventy million Won and only then would I be able to live the remaining ten years peacefully.

If you wonder why ten years, it was because he was going to live until he was eighty-eight, which automatically meant that I could only live to be eighty. It was perfectly obvious that we were going to die at the same moment. So he had calculated that with seventy million Won, we could live ten years with an income of five hundred thousand Won a month.

How on earth had he been able to get that all worked out, when he had absolutely no idea of what money I bought his food with, where his drink came from, or how I managed to make ends meet? At first I used to be amazed too. Whether or not he had any sense of realities, it was ludicrous and almost miraculous to think of him managing even an approximate financial calculation.

In the course of his entire lifetime, the money he had

actually handled went from a hundred Won coin at the small end of the scale to a few ten thousand Won notes at most, nothing more; I was all the more ready to concur whole-heartedly with this sudden 'Ch'ŏn Sang-pyŏng style superannuation scheme.'

'Do you reckon you'll manage to save up seventy million?'

'Don't worry. Seventy million? That's nothing. Make it a hundred!'

'What? You, earn a hundred million? It's not possible. You only make six hundred. Seventy million will do! We don't need a hundred!'

'*Aigu,* nobody would think you graduated from commerce college . . . Why, Ch'ŏn Sang-pyŏng graduated top of his class in business management. He studied so well, even if he just sits back, he's got all he needs for the rest of his life.'

'*Mundunga, mundunga, mundunga,*'

Now and then I would try telling him that I only intended to run Kwich'ŏn until I was sixty, and he would coax me gently.

'You look so young, you'll only look sixty even when you're seventy. Just try telling people that an old sixty-year-old is running a tea-room. A lot more customers will come because they'll feel sorry for you.'

At the same time he insisted that I must save two thousand Won a day and ten thousand on Fridays.

Since his plans for our old age depended entirely on the success of Kwichŏn, he was intensely concerned about how many customers came each day. He would phone five or six times a day and invariably he would ask about the number of customers. If he was in a very good mood, he would ask how I was first, but usually he would demand point-blank to know how many customers there had been.

'Have you had lunch?'

'Yes, I have.'

'How many customers are there? Will you reach sixty?'

'Of course I will.'

'Thank you, ah, thank you! Well done!'

If there had been a lot of customers, he would end by congratulating me; if the contrary was true, he would be upset and hang up, clunk, without another word.

Yet when he actually came down to Kwich'ŏn himself, it made absolutely no difference to him if there were a lot of customers or only a few.

While his health was still alright, before 1988, he would come down on Wednesday and Friday afternoons. He would spend the afternoon talking with the customers, go along to visit the Writers' Association and the *Paduk* Association, then return home.

After he got sick, when his conduct had become rather erratic, I felt uneasy about his travelling alone and he would come down with me to Kwich'ŏn earlier on the Friday mornings.

He had his regular seat in Kwich'ŏn. It was nearest the counter, and he used to lean so hard against the wall that several times I had to re-paper the part where his shoulders rubbed, and soon it would be tattered again.

There he would sit and every time a customer opened the door he would welcome them with his loud cry: 'Come on in. There's room. There's room.'

He would greet friends and strangers alike but there were two kinds of customers he disliked: men wearing glasses and women dressed in red. No matter how nice the face or how well-behaved, he disliked those two kinds of things. If a man wearing glasses happened to be with a girl, he would stare in silence then abruptly address the girl:

'Hey you, girl!'

'What is it?'

'How come a pretty girl like you is in love with a thing like that? Old four-eyes there?'

'What?'

'No, no, it's alright, it's alright. He's a lucky fellow, to have such a pretty girl for a sweetheart. You're sweethearts, aren't you?'

'No, we're just friends.'

'Sure, sure; it'll turn out fine.'

It was never clear just why he didn't like people with glasses. He used to say that when people were reading they kept staring straight ahead and ruined their eyesight and that then they had to wear glasses like idiots and he didn't like that. At the same time he would advise people: 'Look at green things; looking at green things is good for your eyes.'

There was only one young man with glasses that he liked, No Kwang-nae, who was like a son for him.

'People don't choose to wear glasses, do they? Only

look at No Kwang-nae, he wears glasses, doesn't he?'

'True, it's as you say, but with you it's ok, Kwang-nae, you're alright even with glasses.'

With the exception of Kwang-nae, every man wearing glasses who came to Kwich'ŏn had to endure my husband's fierce glare.

Girls dressed in red experienced a similar reaction.

'*Mundi kashina, mundi kashina, mundi . . .*'

When I heard him muttering like that to himself, I could be sure that if I looked around there would be a girl wearing red or with her nails lacquered red.

'Is it because she's dressed in red?'

'Of course! *Mundi kashina,* to come in here wearing red!'

If he softened a bit after grumbling, that was the first thing he would say.

'Look, dear. Next time you come, just don't come in red. Red's the color the commies like, and it's bad for the eyes, too.'

People familiar with his tastes took care not to wear anything red on the days when he came down, they put on other color clothes instead. Any girls who couldn't scrub off their red nail-varnish kept their hands clenched so that it didn't show.

His favorite color was green; if he saw anyone dressed in green he would invariably express his pleasure: '*Ippuda,* pretty.' At home, the floor was green, the quilts were green, the blankets were green, everything was green.

While people wearing glasses or dressed in red got

the coldest reception, the warmest reception of all was reserved for children. If a child came with its father or mother, there was always trouble, because he would roar out, '*Yonom! Yonom!*' in a voice fit to drive it away.

To start with the children would be frightened by his loud voice but oddly enough they quickly became his friends. They easily got on well, as if they accepted him. He would give them a small coin: 'Come over here; I'll give you a hundred Won, come on over here,' and then they would play together until it was time to part.

Another reason why he enjoyed his times at Kwich'ŏn was because he could meet the friends and acquaintances he missed, and collect 'taxes' from them. They in turn made a point of dropping by on the days when he was due to come down, to pay their tax.

It was a widely known custom; he had begun to collect this tax when he was in his twenties, as a means of supporting himself. It was a matter of getting some pocket money, enough for a drink, from his acquaintances; he would demand it quite naturally in a dignified manner, so it came to be known as his 'tax.'

From early days right through, there were different levels of tax. The amount he demanded varied from one person to another. He would estimate the state of the person's finances, then demand a lot from those he reckoned were earning a lot, accepting just a little from those in reduced circumstances. He would take nothing from people he disliked, even if they offered to give. Some people invited him to put them higher on the scale, but if he judged them incapable of more, he would not accept.

I had always seen him collecting his tax in this way, but when we got married, I asked him to stop. For a while he refrained from collecting any taxes but at a given moment he started again, without my knowledge.

'If the wife knows she'll scold me but could you lend me just two thousand Won?'

The tax, thus revived under the name of loans, became such an ingrained habit thanks to his stubbornness that in the last years he even had a bank book where he saved what he got.

'For goodness sake, stop taking that tax. I give you pocket money, don't I?'

'I can't. I have to take it. Then I can put something aside.'

He also explained that his friends would be unhappy if he didn't go on taking it. There was one difference from the old days, in that now he no longer used the money for drinks, but saved it. So when he came down to Kwich'ŏn, he would collect tax from the customers.

'I've got something to ask you. You see, my wife has lots of money and now I've got to buy a book but she won't give me anything, so please, lend me a thousand Won.'

He would start by getting on good terms with the customer, smiling and shaking hands, before asking. People who already knew about his habit would exclaim, 'I'll give a thousand Won in tax,' and pay up, but if the customer turned out to be a penniless student he would refuse to take anything: 'Ah, really? No, it's ok, it's ok . . .'

As a rule he would take two or three thousand Won as his tax from people he knew. In the case of close friends or people he had not seen for a long time, well-to-do people, he would be sure to demand ten thousand Won.

If older, successful poets such as Min Yong, Park Jae-sam, Park In-yŏp, Kang Min, Shin Kyŏng-nim, or Ch'ae Hyŏn-kuk dropped in, he would demand ten thousand Won as overdue tax.

'Pay up, you wretches. Pay off your overdue tax. That'll be ten thousand.'

'What overdue tax might that be?'

'From the old days, I must have it now.'

'But I paid already. What's still left?'

It was always the same story; when Wednesday or Friday came round, they would deliberately drop in for the customary exchanges.

'Give me a thousand Won.'

'Pay a thousand. Pay a thousand.'

'Give me a thousand Won. Give me a thousand Won.'

'You rotten monk, you old scoundrel, you must pay two thousand.'

'I've only got a ten thousand Won bill. Give me eight thousand in change.'

'What makes you think I've got eight thousand? I haven't got it!'

'Suppose you buy a cup of tea?'

'Right, right. I can get tea on credit.'

That day, the monk Sŏng Ryun suddenly found his tax rate raised tenfold, but soon afterwards he gained the very special privilege of being dispensed from tax. He came explaining that he didn't have so much as a cent, and asking to borrow something; on hearing that, my husband offered him two thousand Won.

'Ai, he's got no money, no money at all, when even a wretch like me has some, he has no money.'

When I think of it, I can't help feeling that Sŏng Ryun was a man of far from ordinary talent to get my husband to pay him two thousand Won in tax like that.

Bae P'yŏng-mo was a close friend of his, too; once, when he was in an awkward fix, he tried playing a trick on him.

'Ch'on *sŏnsaeng-nim*, I'll look after your tax money if you let me have it. I'll look after it, take just ten percent for myself and invest the rest in your account so just let me have it. You'll earn a lot with the tax money you entrust to me.'

'Right, right . . .'

'Right, you'll give it to me?'

'You bet. You rascal! When did I say I'd give it to you? Oh ha ha ha! You'll have to pay more now.'

He never failed to match a joke with a joke. If someone tried to tease him by phoning and saying, '*Sŏnsaeng-nim*, I have some tax to pay . . .' he would immediately see what was going on and reply, 'You must talk to my wife,' or, 'Pay it into my on-line account.' The savings scheme into which he used to pay the money he received had no system of on-line numbers.

He would save up the thousand Won bills he received until he had ten of them; these he would duly hand to me, saying, 'Pay this into the savings bank.' If he was given a ten-thousand Won bill he would hand it to me at once. He was intimidated to receive so much and wanted to get rid of it quickly.

The *Saemaŭl* saving account into which he paid the considerable sums he collected in tax also received the sums he got paid for writing and all that soon came to no small amount; it was intended for clearly designated purposes.

He explained that it was destined to form a reserve to pay for my mother's funeral expenses when she died, to give a present to Yŏng-jin when she got married and to No Kwang-nae when he found a wife. That was why it had to be kept separate from the seventy million I was supposed to save up, and not be touched.

## Money for the journey home

Once I was hard pressed for a deposit on the rent for the tea-shop when it fell due, so I borrowed five hundred thousand Won from his bank account. He found that unacceptable, and kept on and on blaming me.

'*Mundi kashina,* if only you hadn't used that five hundred thousand, I would have more money in the bank now. Robbed of five hundred thousand, robbed . . ..'

'Did I waste it? Did I spend it for myself? Isn't it here, invested in the shop?'

'Be sure to pay it back into my account, once the deposit is refunded.'

'Why, of course I will. Don't fret so. If you're going to go on like that, what about paying the ten million it cost when you were in hospital in Ch'unch'on?'

'What do you mean, ten million? Chŏng Wŏn-sik took care of everything.'

'Chŏng Wŏn-sik paid the admission fee, yes, but don't you realize that nothing has been paid for all the rest? How does that compare? Is there any comparison?'

He had no reply.

'I'm the one you're most afraid of, aren't I?'

'Of course, of course.'

It was characteristic of him as a husband that while he knew and cared about how much we had saved up, he never asked to see the bankbook.

'How much is in there?' he would ask, and once I told him, that was an end of it.

In the summer of the last year of his life, I drew out five hundred thousand to buy the *yuja* oranges I needed for making the tea, but without telling him, only confessing later. I repaid ten thousand each day, the girl from the savings scheme passing by every evening to collect the money. She knew how things were, so that if he asked her, 'How much is there in my account?' she would always give the same reply as I did, and helped to cover it up.

The nominal value of his savings was two million, six hundred thousand Won. That still lay very far short of the sum he was aiming at. Every time the topic turned to his savings, he would repeat anxiously, 'We have to have four million five hundred thousand . . ..' Because he calculated that would be the cost of the funeral when my mother died. At first he had thought that two million would do, but then one day he heard on the television news that the cost of funerals had gone up, and he reckoned that in that case it would cost much more.

'It's a disaster, a disaster, I need four million five hundred thousand!'

'Don't worry. Chung Kwang, the 'Mad Monk,' said that he would take care of it if we didn't have enough.'

'No, no; still we have to save up.'

While he was alive, he only worried about my

mother's funeral expenses; once he had got the price of a funeral together, he died himself. On the evening of his funeral, anxious to put all the money the mourners had given us in a safe place, my mother wrapped the bundle of money in old newspaper and hid it in the empty fire-hole of his room. I knew nothing of that; the weather was chilly and drizzly, I somehow felt that up in heaven he might be feeling cold, so I put a lighted coal briquette into the firehole. All eight million Won went up in flames. My niece, Yŏng-jin took the remaining ashes to the Bank of Korea, but they would only give us four million to replace the money that had been burned.

I felt that it was not just a simple accident. It was as if it had been his wish. It was as if, since he had gone first, he had wanted to repay half for mother's funeral expenses.

In his youth he had survived by the 'taxes' paid by friends and relatives, later he had been content with the one or two thousand Won I used to give him to spend; now he had set off on that last long journey with four million Won in hand. But once he reaches Heaven, he'll be meeting old friends, poets like Park Pong-Wu and Kim Kwan-sik, as well as Shin Tong-yŏp and his friend the artist Ha In-do, and as he stands them a round of drinks, he'll be able to boast:

'Hey, you guys, I've got lots of money.'

I feel sure that the money remaining will be quite sufficient until the day I set off after him.

## *'Ŏmma-yo, Ŏmma-yo, Ŏmma-yo!'*

I call my mother-in-law
Mother.
My real mother
is in her grave back home
so I call my mother-in-law Mother.

My mother-in-law is eighty-three
but she's still hale and hearty,
she cooks meals
and does the washing too.

That's why
although I'm really poor
I bought her a washing machine.

The title of that poem is 'Mother-in-law.' It's not quite accurate, because in fact he never called her 'Mother' but always '*Ŏmma-yo*.'

Just as he always called her '*Ŏmma*,' so in the eyes of everyone the relation between my mother and my husband was not so much that of mother-in-law and son-in-law as that of a real mother and her son. For him, having Mother beside him meant security, comfort and care even if she grumbled, she being a comfortable kind of person. Wife, mother-in-law, and niece all lived with him under the same roof, and since he spent most of the time with his mother-in-law, they grew into a warm and completely understanding relationship.

Once Yŏng-jin and I had left for work, with rare exceptions Mother was the only person he had to talk to all day long. Apart from when he was listening to music, browsing through the newspaper, making phone calls, or writing poetry, he would all the time be addressing her with his '*Ŏmma-yo*!'

'*Ŏmma-yo*! What day is it today?'

No sooner had I left for work, than their dialogue would start up, with him asking exactly the same questions he had already asked me. Perfectly conscious that he was asking although he knew the answer, Mother would faithfully reply, after which he would go on to check the temperature, the time, and the weather.

When I arrived home in the evening, I would hear all the trouble she'd had from her son-in-law during the day; then if I asked him why he had been like that, he would say it was because she was so healthy; he reckoned *Ŏmma* would live to be a hundred.

'I know, I know, I'm going to live to be a hundred, you're going to live to be eighty-eight. And even then I suppose you'll be expecting me to empty your piss-pot?'

'Ha ha ha. When that time comes, my wife will be

doing that. Then you can take it easy. My wife will do everything.'

At that point, he would make as if all Mother's troubles were really my fault, and would take aim at me.

'From now on you'll have to do everything. You get up early in the morning and make the meals, you do it all.'

'When the time comes for me to do it, I will; you'll have to go out and earn the money.'

'How do you think I can earn any money?'

'In that case, why do you keep telling me that I'll have to do everything?'

'Once *Ŏmma* is dead and gone, what will happen?'

'When that happens, of course I'll have to do it.'

'Do you know how to cook?'

'I knew how to prepare a meal when I was six years old. And for ten years after we got married, didn't I cook well enough for you? It's only now that I don't cook, because *Ŏmma* does it.'

'Really? My food mustn't be too salty, you know; do you think you could prepare it properly?'

He found all kinds of things to worry about at the thought that Mother might die. There was his rice and food, to be sure, and the need to get together the money to cover her funeral, but it he also insisted that I should master the method of making the quince tea and citrus tea we served down at Kwich'ŏn.

When I opened Kwich'ŏn it was the first place in Insa-dong to serve quince tea and citrus tea, and it is still the only place serving them all through the year. That is only possible because in autumn each year we mix the sliced fruit with a syrup made of sugar, then bury some in the ground, and stock the rest in storage rooms to keep it fresh, as most Koreans prepare their winter *kimch'i.* That means preparing it very fast, using hundreds of both kinds of fruit, a task that my mother has made her own, working away at it in company with all the old women of the surrounding neighborhood.

Perhaps feeling sorry for my mother, who had to do all the housework too, he would sometimes try to help. Once he phoned me to say that we would have to get a washing-machine. He suggested we took three hundred thousand from his account, and that I should supply another three hundred thousand to buy one. He followed that immediately with another phone call to confirm the matter.

'It's a sight that makes me cry. All the other houses have washing-machines; when I see *Ŏmma* doing the washing without one, it makes me cry. Have you bought it yet?'

'Not yet I haven't.'

'All the other houses have one . . . all the other old women! Just to think of *Ŏmma* doing the washing like that makes me want to cry.'

'Alright, I understand.'

My mother overheard him talking on the phone.

'What money have we got to spend on a washing-machine? It won't do. When I'm dead and gone, buy a washing-machine if you want to. And when did you ever once cry thinking about me?'

'I had to say that, so that she would buy one. Else she wouldn't. Ha ha ha ha.'

'Why, how sly can you get?'

Mother told me about it, but still he kept repeating 'it was a sight that made me cry.'

'Is that really true?'

'Of course it is, really, inside I really cried.'

He used the same method to get me to buy a watch for her. He kept phoning, insisting that all the other old women had one, only mother was without, that we ought to contribute fifty thousand Won each and get her one, until at last I bought one. The watch I bought only cost thirty-five thousand but I told him that it had cost a hundred thousand. If he had ever found out the truth, he would have scolded me: 'You bad girl, you must pray God to forgive you.'

He never stopped to think that I was also wearing myself out for mother's sake. Every morning he would urge me: 'You get up. Go on, get up and do the cooking!' while if mother so much as stirred he would insist: 'Take it easy, *Ŏmma*. Tell her to do it.' Until sometimes Mother had to stand up for me.

I called out in a loud voice
to my wife in the room next to mine;
I called and called

but she went on sleeping.
At last my mother-in-law called out,
'What a racket. . . let's get some sleep'

and thanks to those words
I went back to being a loach again
with no hope of even beginning.
(From: 'The Woman I Like')

That poem gives a good picture of how my husband would call me at all hours, regardless of whether I was asleep or not, if he wanted something, but would fall silent at just one word from my mother.

If mother had been hurt, she had only to hear him start his usual refrain, '*Ŏmma-yo*, did something upset you? But you're so good at joking,' to break into a smile again. She used to say that it only took one glimpse of his charming side to make you quite unable to harbor any hostile feelings. She fully realized that when he called out '*Ŏmma, Ŏmma*,' it was no mere habit; he would call out to her as if he were calling his real mother.

Most people first turn to God when they encounter a difficulty, and then their thoughts turn to the mother who gave them birth. His own mother being no longer of this earth, he called for '*Ŏmma*' at moments when he was at the crossroads between life and death.

So it was in 1988. He was very seriously ill, hospitalized with acute cirrhosis of the liver. When he was feeling very poorly, he said that he wanted to see *Ŏmma*. The moment I brought my mother into the sickroom, he began to cry noisily.

'Do you know how much I wanted to see you, *Ŏmma*? Didn't you want to see me?'

'Of course I did. But you know how sick I get if I

travel . . . so I felt I couldn't come, though I wanted to . . .'

She was crying so much she could hardly speak. She spent three days there, then when she was leaving the hospital and he was saying goodbye, once again the sight reduced us all to floods of tears.

He was in constant need of her. He made sure she was always near him, so that she would appear as soon as he called out '*Ŏmma*.' He kept checking if she was there or not. I feel sure that right to his last breath he never stopped calling for '*Ŏmma*.' It's almost as if he wanted to have her beside him when he set out quietly on his last long journey, since he had always felt safe when she was there. She was the only witness of his final moments.

On April 28, 1993, I left home with my usual words: 'I'll be back later' and went down to Kwich'ŏn; Mother was left alone with her great task.

My mother had lost her husband, my father, in the atom bomb attack on Hiroshima, over half a century ago, and now she had to face the pain of losing, after her only son, her son-in-law.

When the moment came, I was sitting in Kwich'ŏn drinking my usual cup of tea after finishing my preparations for the day, without any hint of a premonition. The phone rang and I casually picked it up, only to hear the infinitely ominous words:

'He's collapsed. Come quickly.'

It was the urgent voice of the woman from next door. I can't describe the speed with which I dashed out and caught a taxi. As I sped homewards, my heart was so full of anxiety and tension it seemed it would burst.

On arriving home, I learned he had been taken to hospital, but when I got to Ŭijŏngbu hospital, it was all over. He looked just as he usually did when he was asleep. Mother assured me that he had set out on his journey very peacefully.

It had happened during his morning meal. She explained that he had looked a bit different from normal while he was eating. Anxious that he was eating too quickly and might have trouble digesting, she had been sitting beside him. His single bowl of rice was a very big one, and he was eating very fast, 'You should drink some water while you're eating,' she said and passed him the kettle.

He had taken it, and had just finished gulping down some water when he suddenly slumped forward. That was all.

'Pitiful . . . Pitiful . . .'

Mother wept and wept, just as she had done, clinging hold of him, five years before.

She always used to say he was 'Like a son to me' and that 'He's so pitiful, I can never hold anything against him.' She would tell me that she suffered, of course, seeing how hard life was for her daughter, but when she saw her son-in-law all the time quietly lying prostrate she used to think how fortunate it was that she had such a daughter.

'There was only one person like him in the whole world, you'll not find another. What would he have done without you? I didn't know he was like that when you said you were getting married. I trusted you, and your brother didn't say anything, so I thought he was alright . . . Pitiful, pitiful. Still, once you chose him for your husband, if you had started to swear and say you weren't going on with it, I wouldn't have held my tongue. I would have started swearing too. When I think of the way you've lived, with never a frown, I'm so grateful, so grateful.'

'Why, *Ŏmma,* wasn't he was all the time thinking of you and even worrying about paying for your funeral?'

'Whoever would have thought it. I'm so thankful.'

Hearing my mother's remarks, I was always confirmed in the choice I had made. Mother always trusted me, finding in me a daughter who never once made her suffer or gave her cause for worry while I was growing up, a clever daughter she heard praised wherever she went. It was comforting to think that that trustworthy daughter, having lived to the last with the partner she had chosen, would not be likely to do anything in the future to disappoint her mother either.

That is why I don't mind if I have to hear my mother repeat her remarks many more times, since they only serve to confirm my sense of having done the right thing.

*'Omma-yo, Omma-yo, Omma-yo!'*

# Found under Yŏngdo Bridge

I spent my childhood in Japan. As life goes on, inevitably we sometimes experience good things and sometimes bad, yet in my childhood memories the two extremes converge. There were times when my family lived happily and in harmony in a financially secure environment, and there were hours of pain after suddenly losing our father and being plunged into deep despair; the memories coincide.

In my heart, the film containing memories of my father comes to an end in the year I turned nine. My father was at my side for just over eight years, showering me with love. In the space of a few short years he bestowed on me all the love it normally takes a lifetime to give. I was able to enjoy a happy childhood with an untroubled heart and clear mind, thanks to my father's intense love for his only daughter.

My father, Mok Chae-mun, was originally from Sangju in North Kyŏngsang Province; in his teens he went across to Japan and established himself in the construction business. He married my mother by family arrangement and returned with her to Japan, at which time she was in her seventeenth year.

I have heard it said that father loved my mother immensely. She had duly followed her husband to Japan, but to my mother everything around her was strange and unfamiliar, she wept daily for home. I have heard that when his youthful bride had cried herself to sleep begging to be sent back to Korea, he used to tuck her up in bed. According to mother, he was a good-natured man who understood other people. He was a fine leader, a good talker, and of boundless generosity.

Leaving his new bride at home, he would travel about busily; his general repairs business flourished and he had many calls from a variety of places. It was said that when a conflict broke out in some mining region, he was called to help settle it. Arriving there, it seems, he had no sooner begun to expose the problem in a neat, mannerly way than everyone began to nod their heads in agreement.

When talking of my father, it is impossible not to mention drinking and singing. He had only to sing an air from some traditional Korean song and all the geishas were on their knees exclaiming over how well he sang and how elegantly. He would at times drink almost nonstop, but if he once decided that he was no longer going to drink, not a drop would pass his lips for months on end, so strict he was with himself.

My brother was born four years after they got married. That was a joy they only arrived at after a great fuss in the middle of the pregnancy, so that even now mother looks amused and ashamed on recalling it all. It happened while mother was busily working at the textile mill. Mother's complexion was originally white and pretty; at the time she had a good appetite so that she had put on weight, she was even whiter and plumper than before. Her stomach seemed to be protruding a little, it was true, but she merely put that down to increased weight. She had absolutely no idea that her stomach was swelling because she was pregnant.

One day mother exclaimed in a panic that an insect had got inside her stomach. It was the baby moving but, not realizing what it was, when she felt something squirming inside her she began to shout that an insect had got inside her. She rushed to the hospital, where the doctor informed her that she was already six months pregnant.

She had not lost her appetite, or felt any other symptoms, she had never for a moment suspected that she was pregnant and she says she felt so ashamed of her naivety and ignorance she could not hold her head up. Father, on the other hand, was so happy he could not sit still but went walking about everywhere smiling broadly.

As a result, when his son was born, father at once named him Sun-bok : Innocent blessing. When he was four, father brought his family back to Korea for a brief visit. Mother stayed with Sun-bok in Sangju while father travelled back and forth between Korea and Japan.

He would stay in Japan for up to six month then come back again; Mother tells that every time he came back he would meet 'people from Manchuria' and confer with them in whispers before giving them money. Still today she occasionally reminds me: 'In those days, your father was earning well, and he used to provide funds for the Independence Movement.'

Later a mining operation started up at Changsŏng in Kangwŏn Province, and father was very busy with a big construction project. Once that was finished, my parents planned to go back to Japan, although now, after eight years, they were anxiously expecting the birth of their second child.

I was born in the second lunar month of 1937, when they were waiting in a rented room in Pusan for a boat, intending to return to Japan. Mother felt the onset of birth pains one morning; she got everything ready for the delivery, then at about four o'clock set about preparing the evening meal, earlier than usual. Once the rice was boiling she turned to go to her room, at which point I emerged into her drawers!

The fact that the delivery had gone so smoothly was a great comfort to mother, who had suffered very much from her inability to conceive.

It seems that my brother Sun-bok was full of amazement at the sight of this new-born baby with its pretty little melon of a head when he came home from school.

'Where did that come from?'

'I found her under Yŏngdo Bridge.'

'Really?'

On account of mother's reply, my brother says that all through his childhood he really believed it was true. Anyway, from that day until his last breath, my brother dearly loved his little sister 'from under Yŏngdo Bridge.'

# On my brother's back

Our parents took the two of us to Japan and settled in Hiroshima. I grew up as the late-comer in an economically secure family, with nothing to envy anyone.

'Daddy, I want to wear a hat.'

'Daddy, now I want to visit the garden.'

'Daddy, I know what I want to eat . . .'

I had barely spoken, before father brought me what I wanted, anything I asked for. Once we went shopping in a famous department store in the center of Hiroshima. He bought all the things I selected, until there were no less than four hats for me in the shopping bag.

'If you bring the child up like that, what will become of her? She will be completely spoilt.'

'Don't talk like that! We've hardly any children; we must give plenty to the ones we've got. Without ever being able to give enough . . .'

My parents used to squabble over me, but it made absolutely no difference. If there was something I felt I needed, I would call, 'Daddy' as if reciting a magic spell, and he would act like the genie in Aladdin's lamp, granting all my wishes.

My brother was older, and that much sharper; when his own influence was insufficient, he would make use of me. He used to cajole me: 'Ok-a, why not tell them like this . . .?' He knew very well that my parents would listen to what I said.

In those days too, no matter where we went, my brother would take me about, carrying me on his back. At such moments, when he wanted to play a joke on me, he would gently set me down.

'Ok-a, when you reach this point, I'll carry you again.'

He would say that after having gone a little way ahead and sat down. When I reached the point he had indicated, full of hope, he would have moved on a little farther, playing with me.

'Ok-a, just this little bit more, then I'll carry you.'

At last, after the same trick being repeated three or four times, he would offer me his broad back.

Years later, when I was married, I sometimes used to find myself facing his back again. He was so fond of me, he felt a need to see me every day so that if we did not visit him at my mother's house, he would come to visit us. When he came to us, he used to offer me his back and offer to carry me.

'Sang-pyŏng-a, I'm giving my sister a ride.'

'Really, at her age, riding piggy-back.'

'She may be your wife, she's my little sister.'

Such was my brother, who cared for me so much and went away so soon. Compared to his serious ways, I was a troublesome little girl. I was all the time alert for any chance to play tricks and games, on each and all alike. If there were dried octopus or squid hanging up in the neighborhood stores, I would chew some in secret, throw the rest down, and run away. I also used to shame the local women by asking those with shaking heads, 'Why do you shake like that?'

Once mother opened her mouth so wide I could see her uvula:

'Mother, soon you'll be dead! There's something strange hanging in your throat!'

'That's not strange; everybody has one, it's called the uvula.'

I was frightened to learn that everybody had one, so I dashed out into the street. There I grabbed hold of passers-by and asked them to open their mouths. Even now I find it wonderful to think of all those people opening their mouths and showing the inside at the request of a tiny child. Each time I would check their uvula, then shout: 'Mister, you'll soon be dead. Missus, you'll soon be dead.'

Even after entering primary school when I was turning seven, I continued to be as mischievous as before. I used to love giving people things; if there was anything at home that struck my eye, I would carry it off and present it to a friend. If mother had bought a crate of oranges, I would share them out to my friends, without even my brother knowing. I also got into trouble for giving sweaters my mother had given me to friends, cutting off part of the sleeves, depending on the length of their arms.

Perhaps it was because we were rich, but even when

we returned to Korea, which was then a Japanese colony, Japanese children envied me. For whatever reason, our school teacher from Japan was so fond of me, she came to call for me at home every morning.

In photos taken during school outings, I am the only one wearing nice shoes while all my school-friends are wearing wooden clogs. Given that we ate unadulterated rice even during the hardest days of the Pacific War, that was surely no great luxury.

I was accustomed to the taste of rice unmixed with any other kind of grain and would not touch ordinary foodstuffs made from bean flour or red beans. When we received lunch at school, I never ate it but instead shared it out among my friends.

There was an economy drive at school, and the children used to bring along their own bowls for lunch. The Japanese children would each bring bowls for rice and soup made of bamboo, while I distinguished myself by bringing delicate, high-quality Japanese porcelain bowls, refusing to use bamboo.

At the roadside on the way back home after coming out of school, there was a house surrounded by a stone wall. As I passed by I had the habit of throwing a bowl at the wall for fun. I broke one bowl every time I passed the house.

Mother was very attached to her bowls and had a collection of good quality ones, but thanks to me she suffered many losses. Scold me though she might, I went on breaking three or four a week. If she tried to make me take things of lesser quality, I used to pout and kick up a fuss, refusing to go to school. I really was a little minx, the subject of many rumors.

People say that our basic personality is formed in childhood; well, I spent mine peacefully and freely doing just what I wanted. The energetic side to my character, that sends me forging ahead in all circumstances, is certainly not unrelated to the way I spent my childhood years.

Then in a moment the atom bomb deprived me of my childhood of luxury. It was my ninth year of life. The American atom bomb exploded in a great burst of light and my father, who was in downtown Hiroshima, vanished without trace. Mother searched through the mounds of corpses filling every street in search of his body, but to no avail.

We were living in the district of Kusasumachi, that lay several miles from the center of Hiroshima, so that the people living there were able to survive. I was studying in a temporary school that had been installed in the local Shinto shrine. In those days the war was hastening toward its bloody end and we were not forced to study at regular school; instead, classes were taught in each neighborhood's Shinto shrine.

It was still quite early in the morning, when suddenly I had the impression of something like a flash of lightning, then a fierce blast of wind came blowing. It was terrifying; the upper floor of the building went flying through the air. Fortunately, we were sitting in the shadow of some trees and we escaped without being affected by radiation.

My brother was attending class at the technical high school in central Hiroshima; he had a narrow escape. He was working at a machine in the classroom when he felt a blast of light; taking it for a flare, he went rushing outside and at that very moment, he said, the school building collapsed.

That brief instant was all that separated life from death. Providentially, my brother found himself standing on this side of the shore. We three survivors waited for father, and went out looking for him too. We certainly thought that he must have been killed, but it is very difficult to believe in a death that one has not witnessed, and where no body can be found. Pregnant with her third child, mother strove to find some trace of him, rummaging among mounds of corpses, but to no avail.

In the end we were obliged to leave without being able to verify anything. Terrible to tell, after the atom bomb fell on Hiroshima, we were forced to flee from frenzied mobs of Japanese intent on turning their blades against Koreans in reprisal. After several days of reports that the Japanese were setting fire to the homes of Koreans, robbing them of their belongings, and killing them, mother made haste. She decided we must quickly go back to Korea before anything happened to us, and began to pack.

Luckily, Kusasumachi was located near the sea, it was a good spot to set out from. Koreans assembled three different boats and spread themselves among them; we followed my brother's advice and boarded the largest.

It was just at the end of the war and it took an eternity to make our way among the countless sunken ships. I recall that we stopped here and there to rest, and in particular I retain a vivid memory of the salty taste of the rice we washed and boiled in sea-water, after sleeping one night on the island of Temado.

After we had left Temado and were on our way to Pusan, we encountered heavy seas and nearly perished. The women were exhausted from bailing, while the men were busy tying the deck down with ropes. If water had filled the boat and forced the deck off, we would all have died. Fortunately some of us had had experience of boats, they tied the ropes calmly and prevented disaster. Still, we were lucky to have boarded the largest boat, for if we had been in one of the smaller ones it is not sure we would have survived such a storm. Thanks to my brother's good judgement, we landed safely at Pusan.

On my brother's back

# Swimming through Hell

After losing our father in that atomic explosion, a disaster so totally unforeseen, we set out to run our household once back in our home country without its main support. But we were never again able to live united as a loving family under a single roof, for my brother was already well on the way to becoming an adult and had to find his own way in life. He could not merely pass his time living with mother and me without any goal or plan.

The months from the moment we landed in Pusan until we were settled in Sangju were the last period when the three of us lived together for a comparatively long time. In the winter of that year mother gave birth to my little sister, father's posthumous child. However, in spring the following year the child caught smallpox and died. My brother, now seventeen years old, left us too. He said he was going to visit a cousin on mother's side living at Changsŏng up in Kangwŏn Province. Soon after, he sent news that he had enrolled in the second grade of T'aebaek Middle School, a technical high school.

For the next four years our family lived separated, then we were briefly united in the chaos of the start of the war in June 1950. Our cousin, together with other members of mother's family, left home and came fleeing southwards; arriving in Sangju, he sent my brother to our home urging us to accompany them.

'Escape? What do you mean, escape? We're not going.'

Faced with mother's refusal, the rest of the family continued their flight toward the south-east. But we soon found that we could not remain in safety and just a few days later we belatedly fled southwards to Sŏnsan.

After ten days or so spent there, the North Korean army had advanced so far south that even Sŏnsan had become dangerous. We had no choice but to cross the Nakdong River. Swept onward in a flood of refugees, we were near the river when an American fighter came flying overhead and attacked.

It was a moment when disguised North Korean soldiers had hidden among the waves of refugees and so got across the Nakdong River. The American army had already cut the iron bridge crossing the river at Waegwan and their planes were indiscriminately bombing the boats carrying refugees across, too.

My brother, now twenty years old, calmly led the two of us on.

'Once a plane has finished bombing and gone away, there's some time before it comes back for another attack. We must use that time to get across the river.'

Following his instructions, as soon as an attack started, we went into a nearby field of flax and lay flat.

'Quickly, let's get across!'

As soon as the plane had finished its raid and flown off toward its base, my brother called us. Arriving at the river, we found a scene straight from Hell. The river was covered with the corpses of dead refugees and the debris of overturned and shattered boats. Oxen that had been brought along, and household goods, were drifting in chaos; women carrying little children were being swept away in the stream, unable to get to safety. Even when their husbands were able to get near them, they were still out of reach, they could do nothing but stamp their feet in anguish. My brother paused for a moment, aghast at the scene, then disappeared and returned dragging a kind of raft.

'I'll take the luggage across first, then come back; so don't move, just stay here.'

Having ordered mother to wait, he quickly began to row across to the far side of the river. Mother was silent, seemingly deeply afflicted by all her son's efforts.

'It's going to be too much for him, crossing back and forth again. Let's get across on our own.'

I was by now in the sixth grade of primary school and was a good enough swimmer to get across ordinary streams, so I reckoned I could manage what mother suggested.

Feeling that it would help my big brother, I bravely plunged into the river, but once in the water things were very different. I set out to swim across, holding mother's hand, but while I bobbed along, she kept sinking. Abruptly, sensing danger, mother pushed me away: 'Look after yourself.' Splashing wildly, we drifted downstream as we made our way across and even a slight mistake in our direction might mean we were drawn into deep water where there were strong currents. It would surely be the end of us if we drifted into that; both I and mother kept calling for help on Avalokitesvara, Bodhisattva of Mercy.

I was floundering along when some men seized my arms and helped me stand upright. Standing there, I came to my senses and realized the water was lapping at my chest. I had been struggling on in a panic when in fact I was already across. Mother succeeded in following me over, and we heaved a sigh of relief.

We had made that enormous effort in order to spare my brother, but it all turned out to have been in vain. He had already gone back to fetch us. Being the sensible person he was, as soon as he saw that we were not where he had left us, he made his way back again. At last the three of us locked arms in an embrace and wailed together.

On crossing the river, we learned that we would still have to walk another twenty *ri* by night before we were safe. We walked all night and arrived at reception centers for refugees organized according to which province they came from. My brother stayed with us for over a fortnight in the center for people from Kangwŏn-do, then he set off again. He had enrolled as a student volunteer. As soon he had left at the head of fifteen younger recruits, mother and I set off south for the town of Kyŏngsan.

Kyŏngsan was a place where soldiers received training and, if there were fatalities, their graves were dug in the mountains there. It was as if mother thought that she had to be nearby, since if my brother happened to be unlucky, he would be buried in the hills behind Kyŏngsan.

The two of us found a room in a house attached to an orchard. Mother went up to the burial ground every day. When she left home she would be full of melancholy and when she came back home I would steal a glance at her face, visibly more relieved, with much the same feelings. Mother never once missed a day in her visits to those sorrowful graves. In the middle of all that came news that the course of the war had swung in the allies' favor and they had recaptured Inch'ŏn.

When August came, the refugees who had escaped south agreed that it would be safe to return home. So we went back to Sangju. But the eagerly awaited news of my brother failed to materialize.

Mother loved flowers, and she applied all her efforts to growing cosmos, crape-myrtle, balsams in the front yard. There was a terrace for keeping jars of preserves beside the flower-bed, where every evening I would place a bowl of water drawn at dawn, and pray that nothing had happened to my brother. Mother watched me as if she did not know me, in very much the same way as I had secretly peeped up at her face in the orchard house down in Kyŏngsan.

Once a letter came bearing the address of the battalion commander. Thinking it contained ominous news, mother's face grew pale as she opened it, but it was simply the letter of greetings that the commander used to send to the families of the men in his battalion at special festivals.

In those days I was a schoolgirl, a mere child, ignorant of everything and I did not even realize that the address on that letter's envelope was that of my brother's battalion, so I did not reply. As a result, my brother naturally grew increasingly anxious about us and passed his days in great anxiety.

In spring the following year, I was in middle school by now, and I was on my way home from school. An older girl coming in the opposite direction saw me and called out: 'Hey, Ok-a, your brother's come home.'

I ran so fast that my heart was thumping and the breath stuck in my throat as I entered the yard, where a soldier wearing a revolver and with the insignia of a first lieutenant stood beaming broadly. Stern eyes, a bronzed face: it was my brother, Sun-bok. We were all together after a full year's separation. That year had brought us all such anxiety that it felt as remote and distant as ten normal years.

On enquiry, he explained that he had been named second lieutenant after taking the civil service qualifying examination. As he had been leading his young recruits along, he had happened to see an advertisement announcing the qualifying examination. 'Well, while I'm about it . . .' he had thought, had taken the exam on his own initiative, passed, and then received a fortnight's training before putting on his second-lieutenant's insignia and setting off for battle. He was in the engineers and had come close to death again when they were surrounded at the battle of Injei, but he seemed to be in good health.

Mother's face too seemed bright with relief, after

making so many visits to temples and offering so many prayers on behalf of her son. He spent his fortnight's leave without budging from the house, then went back to his unit in Pusan. After that it was only when we reached Seoul that we all lived under one roof again. By that time my brother and I had both gone out into the world.

After graduating from school in Sangju, I went up to Seoul and began my 'Myŏng-dong period.' There I met again my future husband, whom I had first happened to greet by chance when I was in my second year of high school, and so the threads of our destinies began to weave together, something of which I had no inkling then.

## Knotting our common destiny

No sooner was my brother discharged from the army than he got a position with the company publishing a weekly magazine dedicated to education, *Kyoyuk Chubo*. By the time I came up to Seoul, he was already fully adapted to the ways of life in society. He was the managing editor, and produced the magazine with two or three journalists, and the company president; he provided the illustrations, took the photos, and wrote articles. When it came out, I lent a hand too.

When he had finished work, my brother always took me along to Myŏng-dong. Tea room, *paduk* club, bar, there was nowhere that he did not take me. Following him about, I met many writers, and his friends all became brothers to me. My brother's friends all treasured me, treating me like their younger sister, and for that reason it was quite impossible for any of us to fall in love.

Once I heard that someone had asked for an introduction. The person he'd asked had retorted: 'You're making a mistake, addressing yourself to Miss Mok. I can't tell you how many distinguished people are interested in her. You haven't a hope.' That was the end of that.

Later, the man who had made the request told me: 'In those days there was no way of knowing how old you were.' Sometimes I would be sitting talking with quite elderly people, sometimes I was getting on fine with a very young set, and since there was no way he could estimate my real age, he had simply wanted to find out just what kind of person I was.

Occasionally, there was one of my brother's friends who would come near to thinking of me as belonging to the opposite sex, then have second thoughts and instead formally declare me his sister:

'When I begin to think that I want to have an affair with you, Ok, your brother Sun-bok's face comes to mind. Then I realize that you're my friend's little sister and I can't ask you to be my sweetheart.'

I felt exactly the same. Thanks to my brother I got to know a lot of people, both younger and older; mixing with that wide variety of company gave me enormous help in growing into a more mature person. Yet all the people I met were my brother's friends, neither more nor less than that. Following that model in my dealings with them meant that I was always able to be unreserved and frank. One such friend was Ch'ŏn Sang-pyŏng, but he too did not escape from that emotional framework. We simply considered each other as older brother and younger sister.

Among the literary figures that I often used to exchange greetings with as I accompanied my brother, certain spring to mind: Pak Chae-sam, Kang T'ae-yŏl, Pak Ki-wŏn, Hwang Kŭm-ch'an, Sŏ Chŏng-ju, O Sang-sun.

Not to mention Ch'ŏn Sang-pyŏng.

My brother had a steady job, which meant he was financially more secure, compared to those often hungry writers; if he went to a tea room or bar, he would take charge of the expenses for the whole party for the evening; if circumstances permitted, he might sometimes even pay off all Ch'ŏn Sang-pyŏng's outstanding debts as well.

Ch'ŏn Sang-pyŏng, who was always very explicit about which people he liked and which he disliked, was very fond of my brother. They were of almost the same age, being born within twelve months of each other, my brother in the sixth lunar month, Ch'ŏn Sang-pyŏng in the first. After we were married, my husband was always most respectful towards my brother.

'We're of the same year, really, but although he was born later, I call him my elder brother.'

If I replied: 'But you shouldn't,' he would reply: 'But he is, really; I'm living with you, so he's our elder brother.'

He used to be extremely deferential, replying respectfully to whatever my brother said with 'Yes, yes, yes, yes.'

Likewise, my brother always treated my husband in a warm-hearted manner. If he bought a bottle of liquor, he would be sure to visit him and share it with him, always finding good topics to talk about.

Ch'ŏn Sang-pyŏng used to take me around with him as if I was his own little sister. If he got a ticket to a play or a movie, we would go to see it together, and if he was broke he would borrow his fare home from me.

When we were first married he used to say in a grumbling tone, 'When we take the bus, she even pays my fare; I can't use money as I want to,' and I have only to hear the words 'bus fare' for memories of Myŏng-dong to arise.

'Miss Mok, can I have my bus fare, please?'

'Mr Ch'ŏn, this is money meant for my wedding expenses. I'm saving up in advance for my wedding trousseau. Later, when I get married, you'll give me a big present, won't you?'

'Alright, alright.'

Needless to say, I never got any contribution toward my trousseau corresponding to all the hundred-Won coins I gave him so frequently. It was not only the bus fare; sometimes he would even drink on credit at my expense.

'Miss Mok, I don't have any money today, but I'll repay it later, so will you ask them at *Ŭnsŏng* to charge what I drink to you? I'll pay it back.'

*Ŭnsŏng* was the name of the bar run by the mother of the well-known actor Ch'oi Bul-am. He knew that she was fond of me. I never once refused his requests and that mother at *Ŭnsŏng* never refused to do as I asked her.

'Give Ch'ŏn Sang-pyŏng something to drink and charge it to me, please.'

'If you say so.'

Standing beside me, listening, Ch'ŏn Sang-pyŏng would rejoice every time: 'Here in *Ŭnsŏng* I'm the only person who gets to drink on credit!' And the credit he said he would repay he always paid fully, if money came in.

It was always much the same, and already in those days he had got into the habit of tossing down drink without eating anything with it. At *Ŭnsŏng* he used to empty a bottle of *soju* while barely touching the accompanying snacks. From there he would go on to Songwŏn-kiwŏn and launch into a game of *paduk*.

We often met, it was always the same routine. He would appear in the tea room in his shabby clothes, wipe his face and his hands in a damp napkin, and decide on our route.

'Miss Mok, shall we go and see a play or a movie?' Or else: 'Let's go to *Ŭnsŏng* and use up some credit.' So our route was settled. Sometimes it would be: 'Ok-a, I've written a poem, you must read it,' and he would show me what he had written, so that I saw for myself all his newly produced poems and critical essays. Until then I had simply thought of him as 'a talented writer, but eccentric' and no more, with no particular feelings. He was different from ordinary people, that was sure. He was considered a genius on account of his intelligence, that was based on a prodigious memory and much reading; he had been recognized as a poet while still a schoolboy and now he was making a name as a critic. Yet although he had a remarkably bright mind and heart, in daily life he ignored completely customs that we took for granted and lived entirely as he wished. Since he never looked after himself, his life was a succession of hardships.

It was not that he lived in that way because he was born incapable of looking after himself; it was a path he had chosen for himself. His way of thinking was unlike that of ordinary people. Ch'ŏn Sang-pyŏng was different; you could not help laughing, beginning with the way in which he had chosen his department at university.

He had had his first poem 'River Waters' published while he was still in fifth grade of middle school in 1952, thanks to the recommendation of the poet Yu Ch'i-hwan, and so established his right to be considered a writer. At the very start of his final year at school, he began to hesitate about what subject he should study in university. The humanities corresponded with his aptitude but since he was already a recognized writer, he felt that there was no need for him to study that.

Finally, he decided to follow a method suggested by one of the older students. He would write the names of all the departments except the humanities college on pieces of paper, roll them up, and throw them as far as he could; he would choose the department that went farthest. The result was the business college of Seoul National University.

He was living in Masan, more precisely in Ch'angwŏn-gun, Chindong-myŏn. He was born in Japan, in the town of Himeji. He used to say that his father had been a wealthy farmer who was cheated by the Japanese and lost everything, so he went over to Japan. The second of two sons and two daughters, he was delicate as a child and the grown-ups were always full of anxiety about him. He was born premature and the adults were all the time calling him 'Little High-Brow' and treating him with special affection.

From the time he was three until the second grade of

elementary school, he lived in Chindong; then the family went back to Japan again until Liberation in 1945, when he once again returned to Masan to live. He entered the second grade of Masan Middle School and from that time, despite his poor Korean, he spent his whole time immersed in books.

He used to tell how he would visit a bookstore in the town center whenever he had a free moment, but since he had no money to buy books, he would stand there for two or three hours at a time, pouring over the books he wanted to read. At last one day the owner of the shop called him: 'Student, you, student. From now on I'll let you borrow books, you can take them home to read.' He was devoured with a veritable reading fever, reading books from that bookstore day and night. He said that later he wished he had known the bookstore owner's name, at least, but by that time there was no way of finding it out, so he simply felt sorry and deeply grateful.

As a wartime refugee, he entered university in Pusan but spent more time mixing with writers than in study. He joined with writers such as Song Yŏng-t'aek and Kim Jae-sŏp to produce a small literary magazine, and began to write critical essays with an article entitled 'This I reject and oppose.' His full recognition as a poet came with the publication of the poem 'Seagull' when he was in his second year of university. From that moment he was formally a poet.

For all that, his university studies were not completely abandoned. In the first semester of his final year, the dean of the business college announced that 'five students from our college have succeeded in joining the Bank of Korea without examination,' hinting that Ch'ŏn Sang-pyŏng had not been the last of the five.

Thus his future was assured, but he was not in the least interested in worldly success of that kind. He was already a poet, life as a wage-earner held no appeal for him, and he disliked attending university; so during the second half of his final year he quit school. From then on for the rest of his life, apart from the time after the 1961 coup d'etat when Kim Hyŏn-ok was mayor of Pusan and he served for a year as his press secretary, he never had a regular job.

Still, living off the money he gained by writing poems and review essays, he was always a hungry writer. He had no regular income, and there was nowhere in Seoul where he could establish himself properly, so that from that time on he was always on the move. A visiting guest moving from one person's house to another's, he received sometimes unwilling hospitality.

In that way the problem of eating and sleeping was solved but still what he earned from writing was not enough to cover the cost of his drinks, so his drinking expenses had to be covered by the 'taxes' he received from his friends.

Still, at some undetermined point the relationship between Ch'ŏn Sang-pyŏng and the person supplying lodging or pocket money always attained something of the feel of host and guest.

'You know, when it comes to people coming asking for money, there's no one to equal that fellow for openness.

The others, the minute they come in asking for money, they creep along, trying to sense which way the wind is blowing, and mutter in low voices, while you wouldn't believe the way he shouts from the minute he gets inside the broadcasting station.'

Cho Yu-ro, who worked in broadcasting, liked that openness and became a close fried to Ch'ŏn Sang-pyŏng. There was another friend who, when asked for five million Won, said he only had three million and he would have to make do with that. On meeting that friend again the next day he thrust out his hand: 'Give me the other two million.'

Chŏng Wŏn-sik was a graduate of Seoul National University's medical college, but he too came to be a close friend; in such cases he would only pay his tax on certain conditions. When he held out his hand with a 'Give me some money,' he would refuse to pay up docilely.

'Shut up. Come with me. I'll give you something if you do as I say.'

He knew very well that Ch'ŏn Sang-pyŏng detested taking a bath, so Chŏng would take him along to a barber's shop and only pay his tax after seeing that at least his dirty long hair had been cut.

As he roamed constantly from newspaper office to broadcasting station, from magazine office to publishing company, Ch'ŏn Sang-pyŏng was always perfectly unrestrained and yet completely honorable.

## 'Crazy Vagabond'

Around the mid-1960s, Ch'ŏn Sang-pyŏng's health started to deteriorate seriously. He had got into the habit of going without food for several days at a time, getting drunk instead of eating, and that way of living was a challenge to even his cast-iron constitution. In addition, since there was no one looking after him, he would spend one night in an inn, the next in someone's house, always on the move, which made it all the more difficult for him to get proper meals.

I continued to meet him quite often, as before, but every time I saw him he looked worse, I felt very sorry for him. The only thing I could do to help was to try to protest to the people who were encouraging him to drink so much:

'It's bad for Ch'ŏn Sang-pyŏng to drink like this, so why do you keep making him drink?'

If I came across them in a bar, I used to scold and blame them, since they were only youngsters of my own age, but that did not solve anything.

In those days, he was staying in an unlicensed inn in

Kuro-dong, and the only food he took each day was a bowl of *makkŏlli* and a dish of bean-curd once every two hours from 4 in the morning until midday. As that kind of life continued, he grew thinner and thinner, and at last he started to walk in a kind of sideways scuttle, like a crab. Drink was his constant companion; there was no one who could interfere.

In those days he was inseparable from one other great eccentric, the poet 'Republic of Korea' Kim Kwan-sik, and they were a good match with their eccentricities, two vagrants who reckoned roaming around acting in a drunken manner to be a perfectly normal way of living.

Kim Kwan-sik was a genius of a poet, who had once stood as a candidate in Seoul's Yongsan-ku in the National Assembly elections; he had then put 'Republic of Korea' on his name cards and went around insulting and swearing at all and sundry, to their great amazement, and generally acting as a complete eccentric. Ch'ŏn Sang-pyŏng alone escaped his vituperations. Each of them had been nicknamed a genius, and there seemed to be a kind of comprehension uniting the two of them. He died at the early age of thirty-six and my husband, returning from the funeral, wept and swore because the people from the literary world who should have been there had not put in an appearance.

Anguished wind and clouds. Your guides.
Lightly you came to this wearisome world
and all that you did

was many beads from your breast
bitter dust from your lips.
All that violently disgorged,
seeming ok today,
you're off just as lightly
all dressed in hemp
in your cheapskate coffin.
The thing we dreaded
was not your glass beads
but the bitter dust.
The helter-skelter esthetics
that began thanks to you
have come to an end.
Gentle friends
not up to either beads or dust,
try to be glad,
since you're safe now,
at coffin rites for Kim Kwan-sik
in the autumn breeze.
('Coffin rites for Kim Kwan-Sik')

Perhaps because they had something in common, they seemed fond of each other, and my husband was deeply upset by his friend's lonely funeral.

Another unforgettable friend was the unfortunate poet Park Bong-wu. He was some four years younger than my husband and he began his literary career in 1956 after graduating from Chŏnnam University in Kwangju, when one of his poems 'DMZ' won the spring literary prize awarded by the *Chosŏn Ilbo* newspaper. The two of them became close during the Myŏng-dong years and later my husband recalled him in an essay entitled 'Park Bong-wu, who vented his anger and went mad':

> I was drinking a glass of grog and getting new reserves of motivation for life after making my way through the Myŏng-dong crowds. That poet, Park Bong-wu, unable to rid himself of his pent-up rage, had a hard life, all the time in and out of psychiatric hospital. There was no wedding ceremony, but first they had a daughter, then after a son was born they got married. They decided to hold the ceremony in Pagoda Park, in the middle of Seoul, so there were noisy articles in the paper about it, and I was there too, I remember it all very clearly.
>
> Later the four of them lived in a tiny rented room in Ŭngam-dong; they never forgot how to laugh, they were a family that lived happily together, I remember how hard he tried to be a good father for them.
>
> My wife was very fond of him, and he treasured her like his own sister since she was his friend's little sister. We couldn't help being fond of them.
>
> After that he kept travelling between Seoul and Chŏnju, doing all he could to earn a living but then his poor wife died of breast cancer and he spent the last days of his life in Chŏnju.

Once he turned up in Kwich'ŏn and declared that when he became president, he was going to make Ch'ŏn

Sang-pyŏng the Minister of Finance, because he had graduated from commerce college.

I can't help wondering what kind of country that would have been, with Park Bong-wu as president, who used to contemplate setting up a separate 'Poets' Republic' where you would always be forgiven your mistakes no matter how often you committed them, and with Ch'ŏn Sang-pyŏng as Minister of Finance. He also used to say that when he was president he would give me a house, and I remember that as something sad rather than as a joke.

# Like a shirt under the iron

One day in July 1967, leafing through the morning paper, I got such a shock that I thought I was going to faint. For there, in an article with the headline 'Spies in touch with North through East Berlin' printed in characters the size of a door, I discovered the name 'Ch'ŏn Sang-pyŏng, poet.' Not seeing him around the streets of Myŏng-dong recently, we had assumed that he had gone to rest for a few months at his brother's house in Pusan.

A group of intellectuals including academics, musicians, artists, poets, many of them studying in West Germany, had been arrested as being part of a large spy ring, but people hearing that he was involved in such a thing simply could not believe it. A person so far from normal life that he did not even bother about getting three meals a day to eat, a person who spent his life pickling body and soul in alcohol: how could he be a spy! I was dumbfounded.

The accusation against Ch'ŏn Sang-pyŏng was that he had known that Kang Bin-ku, his contemporary in the same college at Seoul National University and the central figure in this incident, was a spy, had blackmailed him, and extorted money from him; they claimed that he was guilty of extortion and blackmail. None of his friends could even begin to believe such a thing. What we knew was that Kang Bin-ku was simply a kind-hearted friend who had often paid very generous sums in 'taxes' to Ch'ŏn Sang-pyŏng.

Kang's father was a businessman, they were a very well-off family. As a result he had been unstinting in providing financial help to his poverty-stricken classmate, while they were studying and also after they graduated. There was no reason for such a friend to be forced to pay money, and Ch'ŏn Sang-pyŏng had neither the disposition nor the means to blackmail anyone. His friends clicked their tongues, incredulous. All we could do was hope that our poet would emerge as soon as possible from this adversity.

Since I was not a direct relative, I was not allowed to visit him or be present at the hearings and had to rely on indirect reports. It seemed that the people at the Central Intelligence Agency had given him a nickname, Ch'ŏn Hŭi-gap. On hearing that, I felt relieved, reckoning that in that case things could not be too serious.

On the other hand, he was of a sensitive disposition and afraid of many things, so that I could not help wondering what sort of comic tricks he had done out of sheer terror, to have deserved that nickname.

I next met Ch'ŏn Sang-pyŏng in December that year. It was the day he was set free, having been given a suspended sentence. Seen from the side as he sat in his black suit in the Songok Cafe, he looked unchanged. He was talking, in a voice that made the whole cafe ring, of how he had been arrested and tortured.

He related how it had all begun at eleven in the morning of June 25. He had been playing *paduk* in the Songwŏn Paduk Club upstairs above the Songok Cafe when two young men in black suits had approached him.

'You're Ch'ŏn Sang-pyŏng, aren't you?'

'Yes, why?'

'Will you please come outside.'

The young men were very polite, and smartly dressed, so he felt cheerful: 'I reckon they want to buy me a glass of something,' he thought, as he followed them down to where a jeep was waiting.

As the three of them sped off toward Imun-dong in the jeep, he had been thinking, 'Ah, that fellow wants to buy me a drink again,' for he had a friend who worked in the Intelligence Agency who had sometimes bought him a drink.

Only this time it was different; the jeep took the back entrance. He was led to a room in which there were simply two desks facing one another and, unlike other times, was ordered to sit down. After what felt like several hours, a young man came in.

'Do you mind if I smoke?'

'Do as you like.'

Before lighting the cigarette, the young man asked his address. Having noted it down, after a pause the man repeated exactly the same thing again and again. After asking his address dozens of times, he left the room and several more hours passed.

The next question was: 'Do you know Kang Bin-ku?' His reply was, 'He's a friend, we were at College together,' and after a moment's pause the same question came again: 'Do you know Kang Bin-ku?' The questions started to become wider, about why he had said nothing about his visit to East Berlin, and didn't he know he was a spy?

He was astonished to find that when he simply said what he knew, the questions began all over again from the beginning.

'It was driving me crazy, quite crazy. They kept asking the same things, over and over again, dozens of times. Then they hauled me into a room several times bigger than this café, sat me down there and wouldn't let me sleep . . .'

He had been talking at the top of his voice and laughing aloud, but then he said: 'Later, the electric torture . . .' and could say nothing more, only repeating 'I thought I'd go crazy,' over and over again. He said that he had undergone electric torture three times, and had kept passing out. 'They told me to confess the truth about my relations with that friend Kang Bin-ku who was studying in Berlin but I was innocent, I told them for all I was worth that I had nothing to confess, even if I passed out. Later on, he wrote about those dreadful torture sessions in the poem 'That day':

That day, when I suffered
like a shirt beneath the iron,

I can't say how many years ago . . .

That day when a summer bug
tried to shake hands with me
as I perspired by a back window in a fearful house
I can't say how many years ago.

Your flesh and bones all know
which is mightier,
sincerity or pain . . .

To one side
of the heaven in my mind
a bird is stretching its wings in alarm.

After we were married, he sometimes used to tell me: 'When I think of those days, I tremble all over,' and his teeth would be chattering. And he used to say: 'People say that I'm in such poor shape on account of the drinking, but I'm the only one who knows it's not just on account of the drink.'

Yet he was satisfied that he had personally overcome that agonizing torment. There were times when he said he longed to kill 'that bastard who tortured me' or 'that bastard Kim Hyŏng-uk' but he also reckoned that he had won, 'because I know which is stronger, truth or falsehood, even if I stagger when I walk.' He spoke seriously, like a child relating a visit to some strange and wonderful world, and concluded: 'In the cell next to mine there was Kim Du-han, who got covered with shit in the National

Assembly, so I got plenty to eat thanks to him.' He had lost none of his jocularity.

He went straight down to Pusan and spent a while resting at his brother's home, then came back up to Seoul where we met from time to time as before. There was no need of any special rendez-vous, you only had to go to the Songok Cafe to be able to meet everyone.

Once, while he was still in Pusan, I received a letter. If I went down to Pusan to visit he would look after me, and since it was summer, bathing would be nice too. 'Ch'ŏn Sang-pyŏng wrote that? Shall we go?' several friends discussed it but in the end we never went, just sent back a letter asking how he was. Then a reply came to that: 'Receiving Miss Mok's letter was like finding an oasis in a desert.' I realized that with his shyness, he was saying in that roundabout way that he missed me. It was nothing more; our relationship was not particularly close. We were just close enough for him to feel that after not seeing each other for a while he missed me.

In those days I had developed a keen interest in embroidery in my spare time, and sometimes engaged in picture mounting. In 1961, my older brother had married, when he was thirty-one, and now he had a child. The 'Education Weekly' had been closed down during the student-led Uprising of April 1960 and he was working at a weekly devoted to essays on educational topics. Mother had settled her affairs in Sangju and had come to live in my brother's house too, so that our house in Map'o was full of bustling life with the whole family busily employed in various ways.

When we were all sitting down together in the evenings, I used to tell them all about absolutely everything that had happened in the day. If ever I said nothing, the family would follow suit and stealthily observe me without a word. At last my brother would anxiously ask: 'What's happened?' With the result that there could never be any secret in my life, everything was wide open.

Every day I talked about the people I'd met, where, what we'd done, how we'd done it, and as a result my family were as fully informed about the people I met as I was myself.

It was in the late autumn of the year after Ch'ŏn Sang-pyŏng came out of prison, so not very long after our exchange of letters, that we were concerned to hear that he was in hospital. One chilly evening, with fallen leaves lying scattered where they fell, I headed for the hospital with some other friends. The hospital was in the center of Seoul; Ch'ŏn Sang-pyŏng had gone to visit Chŏng Ŭl-pyŏng in his office and he, struck by how poorly the poet was looking, had called an ambulance that had brought him there. The ward was vast, with room for dozens of beds, and so shabby that it filled us with dread.

The after-effects of the torture he had undergone, combined with severe malnutrition, meant that he was in dire need of proper food and rest.

'Ch'on *Sŏnsaeng-nim,* let's go out and have supper together.'

'Right, right, let's go.'

There was no proper restaurant around, so we ended up in a simple Chinese place and ordered seafood with noodles. He ate everything, down to the last drop of sauce.

'Miss Mok, I want you to do some errands for me.'

As in times past, he asked me to buy things he needed, and handed me various scraps of paper containing various memos. Returning late the following evening with the things I had bought, I found he had been moved to a very finely appointed ward.

Chŏng Ŭl-pyŏng had complained to the hospital: 'Who do you take that man for, dumping him in a ward like that?' Ch'ŏn Sang-pyŏng lay there in his clean bed, having just finished eating a can of the supplies some friends had sent in to him. He asked me:

'Miss Mok, when will you be coming again?'

'I'll drop by again tomorrow.'

'My sister-in-law and my elder sister from Pusan were here. They hoped to see you before leaving but after waiting for several hours they just left. Miss Mok, you wait and see, tomorrow I'll buy you a cup of tea.'

Actually, on hearing the name 'Miss Mok' from the lips of someone who had never once mentioned a woman, his sister-in-law had been curious to know just who this Miss Mok might be. I gathered that as she was leaving she had given him fifteen thousand Won, saying: 'You must buy Miss Mok a cup of tea on my behalf.'

That next day Ch'ŏn Sang-pyŏng left the ward without permission and actually did buy me a cup of tea. During the ten days that he was in hospital, I looked after him for about five. Once he began to improve, we would sneak out each evening, drink tea and listen to music.

After he had been discharged, life went on as normal. As before, he wrote poems and drank. One day he dashed off to Pusan, then reappeared in Seoul. After leaving hospital, he had asked me to help him find a boarding house and I introduced him to a place run by a friend I knew well. It was near the main station; he had been staying there for about two months.

On returning from his brief visit to Pusan, he installed himself in a room across the river in Sadang-dong, which in those days was a barren desert. He invited me to come and visit, saying that when it snowed the view was fantastic. One day he came to show me his title deed; for just forty thousand won he had bought a really large plot of land. Since he had none of the sense of finance found in any ordinary person, I have no idea why or with what money he suddenly bought that land; in any case, some time later he simply gave the title to a younger friend and for the rest of his life never again owned any land.

After we were married he used to say in regretful tones, 'If only I still had that land, I'd be a rich man.' He even wrote a poem about his desire to have land: 'I want to own land as well. Min Pyŏng-ha, that I'm very fond of, owns twenty thousand square yards near Suwŏn. . .' If I asked why he had given it away like that, he would explain: 'He was so poor, I just gave it to him.' While he himself was obliged to travel about collecting his 'taxes', if he saw someone poor he would always respond with a 'Here, take this.' He felt that if he lacked money for his boarding house or his drinks, he could always collect some more taxes.

For a while after he left the hospital, his health was better but his life was still being lived at the same lowest level. Liquor took the place of food, he was without even the basic minimum of nutritional intake, and slowly he deteriorated again. Perhaps for that reason, if we see the poems he wrote in this period after he came out of prison, they seem to express the loneliness and sorrow of his wandering life, and to bear the mark of a great fragility:

Today's wind is leaving
tomorrow's wind is beginning to blow.

Bye-bye.
Today's been far too dull.

Like baby rats mewling in a backyard cesspit
tomorrow's wind is beginning to blow.

Hugging the sky
embracing the sea
I draw on a cigarette.

Hugging the sky
embracing the sea
I drink a draught of water.

Someone sat for a while beside the well
then went on, leaving a fag-end behind . . .

('Crazy Vagabond')

To my own way of feeling, there is a series of poems written at about the same time that emerged from a similar sense of solitude:

> Little girl, why are you crying? Because you've just learned something about life? Because something sad has happened, and you've experienced how very much painful things hurt? Yet this fellow here, aimlessly wandering up hill in the dawn, isn't crying . . .
>
> Little girl, you've got a mother whose hand's soon going to open that gate for sure. This fellow here has no door for any such love to open. Don't cry, little child! After all, look at me: I'm not crying. . .
>
> (From 'Little Child')

The more I read this poem, more I am struck by how very lonely he must have been at that time. Friends used to mutter in those days, 'There's something different about Ch'ŏn Sang-pyŏng.' They would often add, 'It must have been the torture.' They pointed out how, although dazzling poems still emerged, he would also dash off poems that were mere scribbles.

Perhaps it was an effect of the same misconceptions, but when I sometimes used to meet him, and he had turned forty now, he would look so unsteady. He had always had a wavering voice, but now body and spirit seemed utterly exhausted. Then from the winter of 1970, we saw nothing of him for a long time. The novelist Chŏng In-yŏng had put him on a bus for Pusan the day before the Lunar New Year in February, and after that for half a year we never caught a glimpse of him. The day before he left for Pusan, he had walked past Chŏng In-yŏng in the street without even recognizing him, his health was so bad. They had talked for a moment and agreed to meet the next day, but they had no sooner met than he collapsed and had to receive emergency treatment before he left on the bus. According to Chŏong, he could scarcely control his movements at all and his mind was very hazy.

I later heard from his sister-in-law in Pusan that from the day he arrived until the following summer he never once had the strength to leave his room but lay there as if dead. He was completely exhausted.

If he had been in Seoul, I might sometimes had paid him a visit but he was far away and I could only wish him well. I prayed that he would soon get better and that we would once again enjoy hearing his cackling laugh and that thundering voice.

The next time I met him was in late July, 1971. He was sitting in the Disney Café that many writers used to frequent.

'Miss Mok!'

I had arranged to meet someone there, and I had no sooner pushed open the door than the familiar voice smote my ears.

'Why, Ch'ŏn *Sŏnsaeng-nim*!'

My happiness changed to amazement.

His face was dark as if dyed in coffee, and his emaciated body, his cheekbones sticking out, his dirt-stained clothes, all conveyed a feeling that was far from normal.

He was wearing shorts and a blue aloha shirt, which was not usual, while both the pockets of his shirt were stuffed full of cigarettes, which looked quite alarming.

'Miss Mok! I'm glad to see you!'

'How have you been all this time?'

'Alright, quite alright. Now I've come back to Seoul. I'll be here tomorrow too.'

'Very well, Ch'ŏn *Sŏnsaeng-nim*. I have to meet someone now, but I'll see you here tomorrow.'

'Right, Miss Mok, and I'll be off now.'

His voice could still fill the room, but the way he walked as he left the cafe was not that of a healthy man. It was clear that he had not recovered properly, but had firmly set his heart on coming back to Seoul. I did not know that he was still so poorly that he had barely been able to crawl about the house in Pusan. It was a wonder that he had made it to Seoul at all.

I went back to the Disney Cafe the next day, but was unable to meet him. There was no sign of him the next day, either, nor the next. His friends were all waiting, but there was not so much as a shadow of him. He was not to be seen at the Disney, that in those days was the writers' favorite hideout, and he did not turn up at the Hanguk Kiwon, at their regular drinking-hole.

The novelist Kang Hong-kyu had met him the day he vanished, at the entrance to the Hanguk Kiwŏn, but he had poured out a stream of such strange talk that he had wondered if he had not gone mad:

'I came all the way from Pusan by bicycle; getting over the pass at Ch'up'ung-ryŏng was the hardest part.'

'On the way here I dropped in on Han Mu-suk's husband and he lent me five million Won.'

After this kind of disconnected talk, they had parted and he too had looked about for him the next day, but could find no trace of him.

We tried to convince ourselves that he had gone back to Pusan but then we heard that his friends in Pusan were anxious about him too, and our conjectures moved to 'missing' and then to 'dead.' After there had been no sign of him for three months in either Pusan or Seoul, that conjecture seemed to be confirmed. We felt compelled to believe that since he had been in such a poor state, he had simply collapsed somewhere along the way and died.

Which is the background to the story of how a memorial volume of poems was produced for someone who was still alive.

His friends sorrowfully lamented over the fact that he had died at forty without ever publishing a collection of poems, and finally decided to collaborate to produce one. The poet Min Yŏng worked hard to collect the scattered texts together, and Song Ch'un-bok willingly offered to look for the funding.

With great difficulty we managed to unearth poems buried here and there and bring them together, but there was no one with any money. Nobody was willing to make an advance, on the grounds that the book would not sell, or that people did not like Ch'ŏn Sang-pyŏng's work. Min Yŏng went to visit a senior poet who he thought could easily provide what was needed, but he confessed that he simply shook his head and, what was even more disappointing, spoke just like famous people always do.

pointing, spoke just like famous people always do. Worn out after all kinds of efforts, Min Yŏng finally emptied his own pockets and managed to get fifty thousand Won together, before turning to Song Ch'un-bok.

'Well, let's try to get a hundred and fifty together and bring the book out.'

Asked to help find what was lacking, Song Ch'un-bok readily agreed to provide it.

'Since I'll take care of it all, and it's only this once, at least let's make a proper book out of it.'

And that is how the poetry book *Sae* (Bird) appeared, bound in hard covers, finer than any volume of poetry we had previously seen. It was December 1971.

Like a shirt under the iron

# Wed to a bird without wings

Whenever he talked about his childhood, there was one story that always came first. He had expected to die and had come out alive, so he called it 'the first miracle God saved me by.'

It happened when he was six or seven. His older brother and some other older local boys said they were off to the hills to cut wood, so he followed them. They climbed far up into the hills and collected enough wood for each to have a full load, then they started back down. Little Ch'ŏn Sang-pyŏng was valiantly following his elders when he lost his footing and rolled right over the edge of a cliff. He only had time to think: 'I've had it,' before he found himself dangling from a branch, alive.

Even when he had passed sixty, he used to say it had been such a hair-raising experience that it still gave him goose pimples. Since he had escaped without a scratch, he saw it as the first miracle resulting from God's decision to save him.

What he called his second miracle came when he had passed forty. Every one had concluded that he was dead, and he came back alive from the brink of the pit.

The memorial volume of his poems *Sae* had been published and was just beginning to become known when we heard the report: 'Ch'ŏn Sang-pyŏng is alive.' Doctor Kim Chong-hae of the municipal psychiatric hospital, who had been caring for him, had read a newspaper report on the book and made the news known.

I first heard about it in a letter from his brother in Pusan. I had written to announce the publication of the volume, and in his reply he told me that amazing news had come from some doctor. Bewildered and overjoyed, I went hurrying to Park Chae-sam's office; he too had just been in touch with Doctor Kim and was about to go and visit the hospital.

'We were contacted by the hospital yesterday. Song Ch'un-bok and Min Yong, Song Yong-t'aek and I are going to visit him there now; perhaps you could go tomorrow?'

'Alright. Off you go now.'

As I made my way home, I felt at the same time relieved and confused. The fact that he was alive made me want to cry for joy, but at the same time, the fact that he was in a psychiatric hospital wrung my heart. What state could he be in, to have spent almost six months cut off from the world? I felt deeply anxious.

The next day, I heard the report of the friends who had gone to see him the previous day and gathered the overall state of things; then I bought some supplies and headed for the hospital. To my surprise, I found that the doctor in charge of his case, doctor Kim, was an old acquaintance of mine. Until then I had only heard that news had come from 'a certain doctor' without ever hearing his name.

'Why, doctor Kim, do you work here?'

'Yes indeed; for a long time now. Won't you sit down?'

He is dead now, but at Pusan High School Doctor Kim had been a pupil of Park Chong-woo, whom my brother considered as an older brother. Moreover, in high school he had been a classmate of Ha In-Du, an artist who was very close to Ch'ŏn Sang-pyŏng and my brother, so we were all on familiar terms. He was no man of letters, but he did write one book, and was deeply interested in literature, so that he had long known of the existence of the poet Ch'ŏn Sang-pyŏng.

He diagnosed Chŏn Sang-pyŏng's sickness as a nervous breakdown. It was caused by malnutrition, just as a machine stops working if it is not given oil. In a nervous breakdown, the system has ways of requesting help and concern; therefore he was not controlling his bowels but simply discharging everything. That was why he was wearing diapers.

The basic cause was the intemperate life he had lived, pouring alcohol instead of food into a body traumatized by torture, so that after too violent a shock there had been no way of avoiding the psychological consequences. Once his body was debilitated, the nervous system had followed suit.

Later, he expressed what he felt at that time:

'I was in such despair that I could feel no hope for myself or desire in life.'

The day beyond
the day I die
lonely in death after lonely living
birds will sing as new day dawns and petals unfold
on my soul's empty ground.

I'll be one bird
alighting on ditches and branches
when the song of loving
and living
and beauty
is at its height.

Season full of emotion
week of sorrow and joy
in the gaps between knowing not knowing forgetting
bird
pour out that antiquated song.

One bird sings of how
there are good things
in life
and bad things too.

('Bird')

It was as if he had wanted to live like that bird. It seemed almost that he had been eager to give up this life and be born again into another one. But although he had nearly given up on life, he was gradually preparing to return, not as some bird but as his true self.

A little later, Doctor Kim brought Ch'ŏn Sang-pyŏng down to see me. With his wildly dishevelled hair, his swarthy face that had recovered a certain pallor, thin as ever, with badly fitting hospital pajamas, he looked dreadfully shabby; the moment he sat down he greeted me in almost a shout:

'Oh! How have you been? How's your brother?'

'We're fine. How long have you been here in hospital?'

'Goodness knows . . . Doctor, give me a cigarette . . . Miss Mok, did you bring anything with you?'

'I've brought some canned goods.'

'Let's have something.'

After he had consumed a can of food, we talked about this and that. There was nothing obviously odd about him, but the overall atmosphere was very different from before. It was as if he was being submissive, there was a feeling of the obedient child about him. When I made to go, he quickly asked:

'Miss Mok, when will you be coming again?'

'Today is Wednesday, I'll come again on Saturday. Is there anything you would like to eat?'

'I feel like some red-bean cakes.'

He also asked me to get him a book of Chinese poetry.

As I left the hospital, I thought how lucky he was. He had happened to encounter Doctor Kim, who had recognized him; otherwise he might have lived on as someone without a past, never knowing who he had been.

When he was my husband later, he used to recollect how, while he was being carried off to the hospital in the police squad car, he kept shouting: 'Do I have to go back to prison?' but that was all he could remember.

As we had thought, that day he had collapsed in the street and nearly died. He never carried an identification card or anything indicating who he was, which meant that if he had died, he would have been disposed of as a vagrant, an ignominious end that he narrowly escaped.

Fortunately a police car discovered him and took him to hospital but he was far from being in his right mind. Asked his name, he replied 'Ch'ŏn Sang-pyŏng' and 'poet' but when he was asked what poems he had written, he could not recall the title of a single one. Since he was completely incontinent, at first they felt that there was nothing they could do for such a wreck and it seems they were even reluctant to take him in charge.

A month later he was transferred to Doctor Kim's service. On discovering the poet he knew in such a grim place, doctor Kim saw that he was in a bad way but had no idea that we were anxious about him and never once thought to contact any one.

Doctor Kim was staying in a boarding house, and would bring a lunch box to work with him; every lunchtime he used to divide up the rice and side dishes and share them with Ch'ŏn Sang-pyŏng. I only learned belatedly that there could be such love, after he had taken in this patient that others had been prepared to give up, and brought him back to life.

I have always been full of gratitude: if it were not for

doctor Kim's devotion, caring for him with such endless patience and affection, he could never have enjoyed his new life together with me as husband and wife.

When Saturday came, I returned to the hospital, bearing as promised the red-bean cakes and the book of Chinese poems I had bought. He had always been a hearty eater, heaping each spoonful high and eating with relish, and the way he ate those bean cakes was no different. He did not simply eat them with relish, he positively wolfed them down in an amazing manner. Of the ten cakes I had brought, he gulped down eight at a single go, leaving just two. Whereupon he opened the jacket of his pajamas, and stowed those two cakes inside, not in any pocket but against his bare flesh, which looked none too clean, beneath his clothes.

'I must take these up to my companion who washes the clothes,' he explained to me as I looked on doubtfully, and went back up to the ward.

Once at home, I began to worry in case he had indigestion from eating all those cakes, but he never so much as burped.

I started to visit him at least twice each week. In theory people were supposed to come just once a week but I found the door was always open for me. I felt it was my task to care for him in this way, especially since he had no one from his family staying there with him, as was normal. It certainly did not start from any kind of feelings of romantic love. It was simply that on seeing this person who was close to me lying there in such a state, I felt that I had to help as I could.

Yet as time passed, warm feelings of affection that I could not explain began to arise. It was rather as though I was happy to be the only person looking after him. Perhaps after all it was the maternal instinct that we women are supposed to have, stretching out to embrace this man. I felt happy caring for him, and he felt peaceful being looked after. It was impossible, yet I gradually felt his gaze becoming warmer as he looked at me.

Sometimes I would go to visit him with another friend, and though we were sitting side by side, he would keep gazing fixedly at me.

'Ch'ŏn *Sŏnsaeng-nim*, why aren't you looking at me? You only look at Miss Mok. Don't you want me to come any more?' My insistent friend would sometimes ask him, and he would burst out laughing.

Now that he had found rest and peace, his health began to improve visibly. When I first saw him in January, he had weighed less than forty kilograms, but by the end of April he was up to fifty-eight. As his physical condition improved, he grew eager to go out. It seemed good to give him some practice at walking, so with Doctor Kim's permission one day we made an outing. He was incapable of walking unaided, I supported him as he made his way out to the front of the hospital and suddenly he was insisting: 'I'm not going back.'

'I won't go back. What need is there to go back?'

'Where will you go then?'

'I can go and stay with friends . . . It'll be alright: *kwench'ant'a, kwench'ant'a*!'

'Alright. Let's go and have a cup of coffee.'

'Sure, sure.'

There was no choice, I told a lie. From the cafe I phoned doctor Kim and prepared a rough plan of action.

'Doctor Kim says you can sleep out if you like, but you must collect your medicine before you go.'

'Really? Sure, sure.'

Ch'ŏn *Sŏnsaeng-nim* unfailingly did as I told him. He rose without a shadow of suspicion, and climbed back up to the hospital.

'Ch'ŏn *Sŏnsaeng-nim*. Wait just a minute.'

While the medicine was being prepared, I quickly left and went home, where my heart ached all night long. I felt sure that he must be feeling terribly resentful and upset, and was ashamed of what I had done. Doctor Kim duly soothed his ruffled feelings, however, and when I met Ch'ŏn Sang-pyŏng again three days later, it was he who was the more apologetic. He had been so overwhelmed by Doctor Kim's admonitions, that he had no thought of scolding me: 'If you didn't return to the hospital, do you realize just how hard I would have scolded Miss Mok, since she was looking after you?'

Suddenly it was time to think of discharging him from hospital. It was all thanks to the care lavished by Doctor Kim and his team, but he seemed determined to shift part of the responsibility on to me: 'Because of you, he's found a sense of peace, and that's made his recovery go much more quickly.' At the same time he kept trying to discover my inner feelings.

'He needs no more treatment. But can you go on looking after him?'

'*Sŏnsaeng-nim*, you know I have no money, nothing, so how can I possibly look after him?'

'No, that's not the problem. You see, one woman is worth dozens of men. There is no one but you who can help him. It all depends on you now, whether he lives or dies; it's for you to decide.'

He had never been adapted to life in this world, even before he was hurt. He was quite incapable of walking through reality on his own. That was why he had led such a wandering life, at home nowhere, drinking endlessly. He had written that once he died, he would be reborn as a bird; now I was obliged to ask myself whether I felt that I could be his partner in the real world that was sure to treat him badly again.

According to Doctor Kim, Ch'ŏn Sang-pyŏng was confident that things would work out: 'I have my royalties, and the land I bought.' He had boasted, completely forgetting that he had given the land to his young friend.

At last, seeing how like a child he had become, I made up my mind.

'Very well,' I said, 'I'll do what I can to help.'

I did not stop to consider what difficulties and hardships might come in the future. As things were at that moment, it was obvious that we had to be together. There was no thought of it being a sacrifice for one of us, and it was not something motivated by mere sentiment, either. It was a highly practical question, involving as it did the rest of our lives, and I chose the path after much agonizing.

For Ch'ŏn Sang-pyŏng, as for myself, the only way

for us to live at peace was for me to be beside him. Just as he would lose his peace without me beside him, so I could never live quietly if I abandoned him.

'I must live for Ch'ŏn *Sŏnsaeng-nim*, there's no one else.' The thought was firmly fixed deep in my heart. For the rest of my life after that, when I was weary or sad, I always found new courage as I recalled the promise I swore to myself then.

In late April 1972 he came out of hospital. As he put on the new clothes and shoes we had bought, he was quiet and docile. I had already rented a room in a small house up near Mount Surak, and we went home there together.

'Sure, no cobwebs grow over living lips. He's a good enough fellow, but he'll never make it alone.'

With those words, my brother expressed his consent to my decision. From his brother in Pusan came the response that if it was simply a matter of my looking after him, he would be too sorry for my sake ever to allow it; he would only be able to entrust him to me with a quiet heart if we were married.

On May the 14th, the two of us stood side by side before the novelist Kim Dong-ni and informed the world at large that we were henceforth husband and wife. The whole assembly was laughing, and the two of us were beaming brightly too, amidst the applause wishing this forty-two year-old bachelor and this thirty-five year-old maid a hundred years of happiness.

There I was, side by side with the man who in his

poems 'Wings' had prayed: 'I want wings. I want wings that will carry me wherever I want . . . God, give me wings, please.'

I had become the partner of this wingless bird, resolved to look after him until the day when he would at last earn his wings and take flight.

# Poverty's no sin

After our marriage, I felt less that he was my husband, than that he was a little child I was taking care of. True, he had left the hospital, but we always had to be careful his health did not suffer and above all we had to find some way of earning a living.

At the start of our married life, early each morning we would walk up to the middle slopes of Mount Surak, and once every other day we would go on an outing downtown. On the days when we did not go out, he would go back up the hill after breakfast, return home in time for lunch, and then write poems or take a nap.

During the wedding ceremony, Kim Dong-ni had pointed at the watch I had given my husband, saying jokingly: 'Your wife has bought you this watch as a way of telling you always to be on time.' As if in obedience to those words, my husband's habit of insisting on eating at precisely the right moment dates from this time.

On Sundays we used to go for lunch to the house of Doctor Kim Jong-hae; at the stroke of twelve, my husband would bellow: 'Mrs Kim, it's twelve o'clock. Let's have our lunch quickly now!' It was always the same, whatever house we were visiting. His meal just had to be served at exactly twelve o'clock.

On the Sundays when we did not visit Doctor Kim, we would eat lunch at home with friends who had come to visit, then go for a stroll in the hills. Since we were always near Mount Surak, it is only natural that it figures so prominently in the poems written at this time. By his poems, he gave Mount Surak some good publicity, and celebrated our very simple home with its thatched roof, too. He wrote poems that expressed the peaceful ways in which he passed his days surrounded by the peace of the hill.

He was certainly becoming calmer, surely because of the relief brought by the fact that he had found a haven and that twenty years of rootlessness had come to an end. Yet it was still true that unless he could maintain this state, his health might easily deteriorate again. Keeping him away from drink would certainly be a problem, but regular meals were the fundamental condition for a settled life. I was responsible for him, and I always had to be on the alert about that.

At the start of our marriage I had to take care of him, for he was still very poorly, and I earned a living by doing embroidery at home. I had been embroidering since before our marriage, so there was no great difficulty about it, but now I had to look after him as well, and I found that there was not enough time in a day. It took a full month to do the work for a single folding screen. Only what with taking him down town, drinking tea, running errands, there was not enough time for me to sit down and work.

One's skill at a job improves by doing it, but since there was too little time, I found I could not work as well and of course our income began to dwindle in consequence. In addition, the work had to be framed or mounted by someone else, and that took more of the total price than it should have, so that earning a living was no easy matter.

When a little money came in, the purchase of embroidery materials came first; then we would buy a sack of rice, ten or twenty coal-briquettes, and there would be nothing left so we would go on for a while, making do with that until something more came in. That was how we lived. Once the rent was paid, the two of us had almost nothing to live on.

Finally, in 1977, a friend and I opened a store selling antique furniture in the Ch'onggye-ch'ong area of Seoul. It was our first experience of business, in a small space we rented inside Hwanghak-dong flea-market. The money had been put up by my friend's elder sister, while a collector who knew us well helped by letting us have a million Won's worth of folk paintings and other objects on credit, telling us to pay it back gradually.

The store was so small that once the wooden objects and pieces of furniture were inside, there was no room left for us, and we used to sit on the cash box. Yet it was the neatest of all the stores, and we had some good ideas, too. We were the first to think of adapting wooden mortars from Cheju-do for use as tables; afterwards it became quite the fashion in interior design to use a wooden mortar covered with a round piece of thick glass as a table.

One year later I set up on my own, but since I had no capital to start with, I borrowed money at high interest from a money-lender and in the end, after a hard fight, I was forced to close down. That was the hardest moment in my life.

During those years there were moments when we had no money for so much as a single cupful of rice. Yet still I felt that the debts had to be repaid; I believed that starvation was better than being despised and insulted. That meant that there was no one I could tell about my problems. I never uttered a word to my mother, or brother, or friends. I reckoned that if there was no money for rice, we could very well make do with half a pack of dried noodles each. I could not stand the thought of talking about money with anyone.

Money is very odd stuff; one mistake and it ruins a relationship. Suppose I told someone of our difficulties, and they could not help? The only result would be that we would both feel embarrassed. Fully conscious of this danger, I never uttered a word about my difficulties. If I had skipped a meal, I never said I had gone without, never said I was hungry.

In those days, my brother had stopped work at the publishers' and was working at home, engaged in making translations from Japanese. They already had three children, it was already beyond his ability to feed and clothe the five of them properly. I had to fend for myself, no matter how.

At that moment someone who had happened to learn of my situation proposed that I take charge of a corner of his store. It involved keeping an eye on the store in general, while displaying and selling pottery and wooden objects. The arrangement meant that if I sold something, I would receive ten percent of the total price for myself. With that, assuming that I made about a hundred thousand Won a month, fifteen thousand would go on rent, a certain sum on repaying my debts, and then I would buy rice and coal briquettes with what remained.

That went on for about a year, then I was able to set up a corner selling wooden objects in a traditional tea-room named 'Tyrol' in Insa-dong. The income was smaller, only about seventy thousand a month. With that amount, once the rent, the rice and the coal were paid for, there was almost nothing left for any bus fare.

After I had been more than a year in the 'Tyrol' I happened to meet Kang T'ae-yŏl there. He had been manager of a publishing company and in those days he had his eye on the room now occupied by 'Kwich'ŏn' with the idea of making it into a shop.

At first I thought he meant one doing the same line of business as I had in the 'Tyrol' but finally the situation became clearer, for he invited me to start up a business in the room he had chosen and kindly lent me three million Won: 'Think of it as *makkŏlli* money for old Ch'ŏn' he said, telling me to take my time repaying it.

That was the origin of 'Kwich'ŏn'; thanks to the kindness of that one person, I was able to be my own boss, incomparably better off than before.

Yet in the twenty and more years we spent together, my husband never showed the slightest interest in how his wife managed or what she did to buy the rice. Even when pains and sorrow were in full flood, he remained utterly serene as if there was nothing at all the matter. So long as he had a bottle of *makkŏlli* and a packet of cigarettes, he envied no one, and so long as he had a wife, he reckoned that all happiness lay in my hands.

> I feel fairly happy this morning,
> with a cup of coffee, enough fags in the pack,
> breakfast eaten and still the bus fare left over.
>
> I feel fairly gloomy this morning,
> though I'm not short of small change,
> because I have to worry about tomorrow.
>
> Poverty's my full-time job
> but if I can hold up my head in this sunshine
> it's because the sunshine has no bank account either.
>
> My past and future
> my dear sons and daughters,
> sometimes come to my grass-grown grave and say,
> here sleeps a life that took pain in its stride,
> let the fresh breeze blow. . . .
>
> ('My Poverty')

He lived exactly as this poem describes. And because he was like that, I became stronger. His eyes expressed happiness as he looked at me, and that was enough to make me forget all my fatigue.

# War Against Drink

One of the hardest parts about living with him was the constant battle against alcohol.

Drink!

Indeed, drink pursued him so tenaciously throughout his life that without it there would be precious little to tell. I had promised myself that I would take good care of him for the rest of my life, and in order to protect his health I was obliged to fight over and over again against drink. In order to keep him off the bottle, I used anger, tears, and punishments, but either because it was beyond human strength or because I lacked what it took, my unaided efforts were unavailing. He ruined his health with drinking and it was only after he had incurred what he himself termed 'God's punishment' that he finally turned into a moderate drinker.

When he left the hospital, he had promised Doctor Kim and myself never to drink again, and for a while he showed no interest in liquor. The main problem in those days was keeping him away from the temptations surrounding him directly or indirectly.

The date for our wedding had been fixed, then one

week before the day, we went down to Pusan. That evening there was a lecture by An Chang-hyŏn, who was a close friend, at Pusan Women's University. During his talk he had given us an impassioned welcome: 'Ch'ŏn Sang-pyŏng *Ssi,* who was dead and has come back from the dead, has come down to visit us together with his fiancée, today is truly a happy day.' Normally, on an occasion like that we would of course all have gone on from there to share a drink together, but that was not for us. When the invitation came to join the party afterwards, I refused, explaining that if we went he was bound to drink and he must not. His warm-hearted friend tried to argue: 'Surely it will be alright, so long as he doesn't drink?' and I was obliged to keep refusing, resisting until it was time for us to come back to Seoul, which made me feel unhappy too.

Then a couple of days after the wedding we found ourselves back in Pusan again, to join in the memorial offerings for his mother. I was busy helping prepare the food, yet my husband kept on at me to go to see a film together, refusing to give up although I pointed out that I was preparing the offerings, so I didn't see why was he keeping on like that.

Since he persisted in his demand that we go to see a film, with all the other adults looking on, we ended up going, though I felt very odd coming back in from the cinema on the evening before offerings were to be made. At least he showed no sign of thinking about liquor, perhaps because of the ceremony there was going to be. It was another matter the next day.

We went out to Haeundae beach to take the air, and that naturally made him feel quite different. We emerged from a hotel after a cup of coffee and were walking across the beach when he sat down under a beach umbrella and suggested we have our picture taken. Soon we had the snapshot, and as he looked at it, he murmured: 'I'm nothing at all to look at, how come you're so pretty? so pretty? so pretty?' He was happy. But as we made to leave he suddenly added: 'I feel like a glass of *soju*.'

'No, you mustn't, Ch'ŏn *Sŏnsaeng-nim*.'

'Just one glass, what's wrong with that?'

'No, you mustn't, not *soju*, no.'

'But I feel like one . . .'

'I told you, you mustn't touch *soju*.'

'Still, I feel . . .'

'If you're going to keep on like that, do as you please.'

I walked away angrily, so upset that I was crying.

'After all, he's so fond of liquor, and he says he'll only drink one glass . . .'

But I knew that if I weakened, liquor would have him in its clutches again, so I steeled myself. If someone starts to drink one glass, soon it's 'one more' then 'a couple more,' for drink has the power to make people think they can break with it, until the day comes when the liquor has consumed that person completely. I encouraged myself, not unaware of that fact, and suddenly he came after me, calling out: 'I won't drink, I won't drink, let's go together, let's go together.'

After we returned to Seoul, for about two months he

never mentioned drink. But when he went down into the town and met his friends the temptation must have been hard to resist.

Once we arrived at the Apollo tea room where we found several friends assembled. It looked as if they had agreed to go out drinking, for suddenly they suggested I wait there for a while and began to leave, taking my husband with them. As he was going out with the writer Na Pyŏng-jae, now deceased, he insisted that he must not drink.

I waited for a while but no one came back. I followed my intuition and set off for the *makkŏlli* bar in Samgak-dong, where I found them all sitting in a circle. He had a glass standing in front of him and was taking his medicine.

'I'm afraid of the wife, I can't drink.'

'Old Sang-pyŏng's no fun when he's not drinking.'

'How can anyone change so?'

They were all having a great time encouraging him to drink. I snatched away the bottle. Na Pyŏng-jae spoke in what he meant to be a soothing manner: 'What about just one glass?' and I felt obliged to be disagreeable.

'Na *Sŏnsaeng-nim*, do you really not want to see us ever again? Is that any way to treat a friend who knows he must not drink even though he wants to?' As I marched out, full of feelings of disappointment, my husband followed me: 'I'm not drinking, I'm not drinking, I didn't drink a drop.' Soon we were back sitting in the Apollo, when Na Pyŏng-jae came rushing in.

'Why, it's the first time I've ever seen you angry.'

'If you try to make him drink when you know quite well that he mustn't, what do you expect?'

'We only wanted him to drink a glass or two, not a lot, after all.'

'No, even one glass is too much.'

'Not a single glass.'

Still, it was not long before the promise I had obtained from him at our marriage was broken. It was impossible for me, who had played the role of a scolding wife in front of his friends, to go on depriving my husband of his fun. Since he was spending a lot of time at home, he was often bored, and so his thoughts began to turn to drink.

'Just one glass!'

Faced with his persistent demands, I found myself obliged to strike a compromise.

'Promise me, now, promise that you will be content with just one glass a day.'

So it was that he was allowed to drink one bowl of *makkŏlli* a day. There was no bar anywhere near our house, the nearest was a fifteen minute walk; invariably at the stroke of noon he would leave home, drink his glass of *makkŏlli*, and return.

One day, as I was on my way home, I happened to see him going into another bar, five minutes farther down the road.

'Why don't you go to the nearer one?'

'I don't like it.'

'Why do you go to a bar that's farther away? Might it be because there's a pretty bar-lady there?'

'Bar-lady? What do you mean, bar-lady? I go there because they use bigger glasses for *makkŏlli*!'

Once he had found a bar that used slightly bigger glasses, after a few months he began to insist on 'two glasses a day.' It meant drinking one glass at midday, coming home, then going for a second glass at three. Since he had to walk for about twenty minutes for each glass, it was a way of giving him exercise. *Makkŏlli* was the only liquor he would drink.

One day early in the morning I was wakened by the sound of someone outside. The kitchen lay just behind the door and as I quietly observed I saw my husband bringing in a street-sweeper, and making him sit down beside the kitchen range.

'My wife has to sleep. So we won't go inside, we'll drink here.'

I lay with my eyes shut, pretending to be aware of nothing. It looked as though he had got to know the fellow at the bar. Every morning he used to go walking in Mount Surak, leaving home at six, returning at seven, and sometimes he would drink a glass with the sweeper.

For the next few times I pretended to be unaware, then one day told them sternly to be quiet so early in the morning, the house owner's family were all still asleep, and soon after the early morning *makkŏlli* parties ceased.

Once liquor had started to pass his lips again, he kept wanting to drink more. The two glasses became three, and he would 'filch money from the wife's handbag' while I was asleep, drink, then write poems about how good he was feeling.

As his intake slowly increased, I threatened to punish him if he went on drinking by depriving him of one of our regular outings down town, and going on my own. Since his drinking was at stake, he opted for that degree of punishment. It must have been hard for him to endure the empty hours until I came back, but the attractions of drink were all the time getting stronger.

At which point he found himself back in hospital on account of drink. In order to break him of his drinking habit, which grew and grew once he had broken the initial promise not to drink at all, Doctor Kim and I had found a variety of possible measures; in the end we gave him some medicine designed to stop him drinking, but it produced unfortunate side effects.

As he began to drink more and more frequently, I recalled a remedy that the novelist Ha Kun-ch'an had once recommended: 'I used to drink too much, but after I had taken that medicine, I found I could not stand so much as the sight of liquor.' Then a letter came encouraging me to recommend it to my husband.

After obtaining Doctor Kim's consent, I gave him the remedy mixed in water so that he did not suspect anything. Low and behold, soon he was saying, 'The drink tastes odd, I can't swallow it,' and no longer drinking. For a short while I rejoiced alone, but then trouble came and that was an end of it. It happened when a friend got my husband to drink whisky.

Originally the remedy against drinking was supposed to remain effective for several months once taken; it was said to wean a person from drink by making them feel nausea and discomfort whenever they drank. But this friend, not knowing that my husband had taken the remedy, insisted that he keep on drinking, and that provoked side effects.

He was unable to sleep properly and began to rave. He talked nonsense for a whole day, without regaining his senses. Finally he had to be readmitted to the Municipal Asylum, where Professor Kim worked, for two more months. During that time he wrote a poem saying that he would not drink again, regretting that he had fallen back into his old drinking habits. The hospital bill came to some three hundred thousand Won in present-day terms and there was no other way but to pawn the gold ring and necklace my husband's family had given me as a wedding present.

After leaving the clinic, he did not drink at all for several months: 'You want to go back to hospital?' was enough to immunize him against any inclination to have a drink. As a result he put on weight, going up to nearly sixty kilos. He used to go down into town twice a week, play *paduk* at the Hankuk Kiwŏn, then meet me at the usual tea room and we would go home together.

In the *paduk* parlor he would meet his close friends: the poet Park Jae-sik, the late Insa-dong philosopher Min Pyŏng-san, the poet Shin Dong-yŏp and others, and that was the time when he started collecting his taxes again. For a while after our marriage he had stopped but then, unbeknown to me, he had begun again to receive fifty Won here, a hundred Won there. I realized he could easily use that money to buy himself a drink, so once again I lifted my prohibition.

In those days we were living in a house where twelve families were renting rooms and nearby was a bar called 'Taegu House' where they sold *makkŏlli* for fifty Won a glass. That was expensive, so every morning I would go out to a store in Hwanghak-dong and buy half a measure of *makkŏlli* for him. That provided three or four glassfuls at rather less expense. If he wanted to drink more than that, I would demand another fifty Won.

If he had no ready cash, he would drink on credit, until I went to the bar and begged them not to let him have credit, so if he drank a glass or two there he would pay for them on the spot. If he only drank that much, there was no risk of his getting drunk, so I shut my eyes if he drank one or two extra glasses. From time to time, I would suddenly ask: 'You've been drinking, haven't you?' and he would answer quite frankly: 'Hmm, just one glass.'

He would spend the whole day in the company of his half measure of *makkŏlli*, good friends together. After breakfast, I used to go out to the shop while he stayed home, drinking a glass when the thought came to him, writing poems, listening to music. After eating the lunch I left ready for him, he would drink again if there was any *makkŏlli* left, and if it had all gone he might buy one or two more glasses on credit, or with his tax money.

If he got bored with that, he would go out to the Hankuk Kiwŏn and hang around the people playing or phone me on the phone of the store beside mine: 'Come out to the Yujŏn tea room and buy us a cup of tea!' In that way we sometimes met during the daytime, or he would turn up at the store in the evening and we would make our way home together.

He was really fond of *makkŏlli*. On Sundays he used to have breakfast at the home of the novellist Ch'ŏn Sŭng-sei, then they would go to take tea at the 'Mountain Path' tea-room near the entrance to Tobong Mountain. His companion always used to drink a glass of herbal whisky there but my husband would explain 'I only drink *makkolli*' and never touched it.

I like a drink
but *makkŏlli* and beer are all I can take.

If I buy one bottle
of *makkŏlli* in the morning
then only drink a little glass
when the thought strikes me
it lasts the whole day, almost.

Beer?
If I happen to get paid for writing something
I buy just one glass costing five hundred won,
yet my wife
disapproves if I drink even once
in a month or more.

That's not how the world is.
At mealtimes

when that's the only pleasure
I feel
how on earth can she pretend to disapprove
of my only source of pleasure?

That's not how the cosmos is,
not how the world is
not how life is.

The aim is only pleasure
pleasure's life's greatest goal.

*Makkŏlli*'s no mere drink
it's the same as food
which is not simply food
but God's divine grace
and gives pleasure too.
('Makkŏlli')

This poem in praise of *makkŏlli* was written when his daily half measure had grown into a full measure, and expresses perfectly the tone of his life at the time.

Unlike other steady drinkers, he never drank *soju*. The *makkŏlli* he normally drank was gentle to the taste, nourishing, and after he had drunk it he felt full and happy, but in actual fact the liquor he preferred above all was rice wine. It was so expensive that he could only savour it if he had been paid for writing something.

Once he wrote an essay about drinking. In it he wrote that, like everybody else he drank 'to forget for a while the weariness of the world,' to forget the storms and hardships of this sea of troubles called life. However, unlike before we were married, he never once drank to the point of drunkenness. He used to call that 'a vice' and hated it. I suppose it was on account of the nightmare of his youth when he had so nearly destroyed himself with drinking.

If one drinks just a little the result is merriness, so he used to call liquor the solution to a wretched life, but even the little he drank slowly poisoned his system, until he found himself once again at the gateway of death.

# As low as low can be

One morning early in November 1987, I was helping him put his socks on as usual, when I noticed that his feet were swollen.

'Why, how come your feet are so swollen? Do they hurt?'

'*Kwench'ant'a*. I'm alright, I'm alright.'

'You ought to go to the hospital!'

'*Kwench'ant'a*. I'm alright, I'm not sick, I'm not sick so why should I go to the hospital? I won't go!'

'That won't do. Why are they so swollen? You really must go. There's something wrong.'

I felt apprehensive, my heart was beating fast. I had already noticed recently how big his stomach was getting, and had been happy to think that his condition must be improving, but seeing now how his feet were swollen, I guessed that there must be some connection.

Mother and I were so anxious that he promised to go to the hospital on the next day, a Saturday. At that time he had been living for nearly three years on nothing but *makkŏlli*. *Makkŏlli* had become his only food. One day he had refused to eat, and stopped taking solid food altogether; he lived on two measures of *makkŏlli* a day.

He was determined to consume nothing else, and the most I could do was to get him drink some of the powdered milk usually given to babies, mixed with water in a cup. Two measures of *makkŏlli* and two bowls of milk made up his entire daily consumption of food.

One glass of *makkŏlli* an hour, one cigarette every thirty minutes, one bowl of milk morning and evening, the quantities and timetable were established and respected precisely. He was quite happy, and used to remark: 'Odd, isn't it? I only drink milk and *makkŏlli*, yet I still shit every day.'

With his diet of milk and *makkŏlli*, he spent his time listening to music, writing poems, then on Fridays he would come down to the town, and visit Kwich'ŏn; he used to say that with a life like his, there was no one in the world he need envy for anything. Then trouble came with a bang, after three years of living like that.

The next morning, as I was getting him dressed for our visit to the hospital, I found that I could not do his trousers up, his belly was too big. The previous week when he had come down to Kwich'ŏn it had been alright. His waist had expanded ten centimeters in a week.

My nerves were on edge as I brought him to the Central Hospital beside the Secret Garden. Our friend No Kwang-nae had made an appointment and he was examined by the doctor-in-chief, another Doctor Kim.

'Well I never! Why have you brought this patient here? There's a liver specialist just up the road at Seoul National University Hospital, go and get him to examine him. Take him to the emergency room and have him admitted at once.'

Doctor Kim merely applied his stethoscope to his belly, spoke those words, and put an end to his inspection. I was speechless, it was my husband who asked:

'Why, you mean it's hopeless?'

'No, not like that . . . but our hospital isn't equipped properly, so I'm advising you to go to Seoul National University Hospital.'

We made our way outside, and sat down outside the hospital for a moment, quite at a loss. He suddenly glimpsed a little child trotting along holding its mother's hand and murmured, '*Yonom, yonom, yonom,*' quite happily, oblivious of the rest. People like him, even when they are utterly devoid of all strength, seem incapable of worrying about themselves.

I sat facing a sixty-year old man.
Don't worry. Relax.
But still, what must I do?
We'll just have to wait and see. . . .

My completely unseen liver
has dared to stage a coup d'état.
There's not much that little fellow can do
yet a life still eager to live comes home to me.

I don't much like coups d'état.
I ask the old doctor
how to deal with it.

Policies depend on situations!
('Liver revolt')

As he had already written years before in that poem, even when his liver finally staged its revolt, he remained serene and unconcerned from beginning to end. I went back home with this husband of mine and Kwang-nae. It was Saturday, it would be hard to get him into the hospital and besides, there was no way we could raise the necessary money.

That evening I called a specialist in oriental medicine and had him examine his pulse. It was a very famous doctor who had been recommended by one of my husband's friends, and who was fond of my husband. Seizing his arm, he exclaimed: 'There's a lot of power in this arm!' and reckoned that he could cure him in a month; he left behind five packs of herbal medicine. After taking that, my husband began to eat solid food again, for the first time in three years.

After he had been taking the medicine for three days, he developed severe diarrhoea. According to the doctor that was the only way by which to reduce the dropsy in his abdomen. He went on taking the herbal medicine for a full month and every day he went to the toilet dozens of times with diarrhoea. All day long mother had to be there with the pot. As soon as he said, '*Ŏmma!*' she would come running and the same exercise was repeated a dozen times in a day.

In the evenings I took over. I would be wakened from sleep eight or nine times, so I could hardly sleep properly at all and in the daytime down in Kwich'ŏn my head was completely fuzzy.

After forty days of constant diarrhoea, he was nearly prostrate with exhaustion, but he resisted. His stomach, which had been taut, had grown a little bit softer with all the diarrhoea but after a while it began to swell again. And not only his belly, but his feet and his scrotum too were swollen. Especially his scrotum, full of water like a balloon, was so painful that if it touched anything, it made him leap. He could not lie on his side and as he was always in diapers, if they touched him he would jump, swear and scold us.

The oriental medicine doctor had been away in Kangwŏn Province and when news belatedly reached him he came rushing back. He stood gazing at his patient as if trying to sense his energies, then suddenly left. A little later his wife phoned me anxiously: 'What's the matter? My husband can't stop crying.' He had been so sure he could save him, it was someone who ought to live but his state was so serious that he had been struck dumb and now he could only cry.

I realized that if it was bad enough to make a doctor weep, my husband's state must really be dangerous. Filled with despair, I found it very hard to decide what to do. I had heard reports that an old college friend of my husband's, Doctor Chŏng Wŏn-sŏk, was now in charge of the Municipal Hospital in Ch'unch'ŏn, to the north-east of Seoul, and after a few days of indecision I went hurrying to see him.

'I reckon he only has another ten days or so to live. I

want him to be in hospital, whatever happens.'

'What, have the old fellow died? Quickly, bring here.'

January 7, 1988, the whole world seemed full of the optimistic spirit of the New Year season; our house alone lay full of a melancholy, sorrowful atmosphere. We prepared to take my husband to Ch'unch'ŏn; he was swathed in diapers, over which we pulled a pair of baggy Korean trousers, then we wrapped him in a blanket. We could find no words, but the whole family was feeling utterly hopeless.

An older friend of Kwang-nae's, a Mr. Kim who liked my husband's poems, had offered to drive him to Ch'unch'ŏn. He explained that his own father had died of liver failure, but when he caught sight of his passenger he seemed to be struck dumb, he could not say a word.

We hurtled toward Ch'unch'ŏn, ignoring every traffic light. Once we had got out of the car, Mr. Kim exchanged a few words with the specialist, and sped away with a parting, 'Let me know if anything happens.' I had the impression that he felt sure my husband was going to die and was upset on that account.

All the way to Ch'unch'ŏn in the car I prayed to God in my heart. At the thought that this might be the end, I was filled with bitter grief. Twice in his youth he suffered and came close to death but if those trials were not enough, please, let him overcome this one too and live at least five more years: that was the prayer I offered.

We made our way to the emergency room and after a while Doctor Chŏng came in. Seeing his old friend after all those years in his present guise, my husband forgot how sick he was and shouted out in a loud voice, weeping copiously: 'Chŏng Wŏn-sŏk! What a time it's been. Ten years at least, since I saw you?'

'You old rascal, what's wrong with your stomach now?'

'I don't know. I really don't know why my stomach has gone like this.'

'Perhaps you're pregnant? I reckon it's twins, you're going to have twins.'

'Hi hi hi, maybe so. I'm going to have twins. My wife hasn't had any kids, and I'm going to have twins! Here, is it really ten years since we met?'

'You scoundrel, what do you mean, ten years? We met just a few years back.'

'How did my wife find out about you being here?'

My husband had begun this happy reunion by crying but now he was gleeful like a little kid, laughing away gaily. All those present were looking at him and thinking: in a week's time he'll be dead. Only he had no idea of any such thing, and went chattering on like a child.

After a precise examination, thanks to Doctor Chŏng he was given a bed in a private suite. Once all the formalities were completed, I felt a little calmer. He was diagnosed as suffering from cirrhosis of the liver.

Treatment started at once. There too they began by giving him laxatives. His diapers had to be changed forty times a day but as a result his stomach grew softer and the discomfort decreased.

During that time, he kept reading all day long. Propping *The General's Son* on his mountainous belly, he read avidly. I don't know how many pairs of glasses he broke during his stay in hospital. He insisted on keeping his glasses at a level with his arms and then he had only to forget and turn over for them to be crushed. I kept putting them above his head but soon he would shift them back to within arm's reach and they would get broken again.

The Venerable Haewuk from Pongdŏk Temple came visiting whenever she had time and on hearing of the problem, she too bought a new pair of glasses for him. She had an attractive face and my husband was very fond of her. He kept telling her: 'You look so wise. You're really pretty. Really wise.'

Although he was so sick, he had recovered his appetite. He consumed quantities of rice, fruit, juice, and would get through two bowls of the laver soup the hospital provided. Normally it was reserved for newly delivered mothers, but he received it by special prescription.

Perhaps because he was eating well, he grew stronger and kept talking in a loud voice. If the door was open, he was kept busy greeting the people passing, the patients on the other side of the corridor, and their relatives. Very often people dealing with him were also embarrassed by that loud voice of his.

'Doctor, I'm giving you a lot of trouble. I'm giving you trouble, aren't I? When will my stomach be better?'

At the hour of the morning rounds, the doctors would enter and he would greet them with imploring tones. But once they had finished inspecting him and had gone out, closing the door, he would curse them roundly.

'You band of good-for-nothings! What kind of doctors are you, incapable of making me better! Good-for-nothings!'

The room next to his was the nurses' station and they could hear him clearly, but he would simply say, 'I don't care,' and go on swearing.

Seeing his strength returning in that way, I gradually regained some degree of hope. There was a remarkable improvement from the first day, and he spent his time without particular problems now he was feeling better.

All that time I also had to keep Kwich'ŏn open, so Kwang-nae and I took turns in watching him. I would go to Ch'unch'ŏn in the evening, relieve Kwang-nae and sleep there, then the next day at lunchtime Kwang-nae would return and I would go back to Seoul. I alternated, sleeping in Seoul one day and in Ch'unch'ŏn the next.

On Sundays, friends and young people who were fond of him would come to Ch'unch'ŏn partly to visit him and partly to enjoy themselves. While I was absent a neighbor in Insa-dong, Hae-rim, helped me to look after things in Kwich'ŏn.

Kwang-nae, treating the younger doctors like a band of friends, even went out drinking with them. One of the interns told him that because of my husband he was applying for the internal medicine section. He had been an admirer of his poems since he was a student, and seeing his name among the patients had made him apply.

At the time he was first admitted, my husband was nothing but skin and bones, and that made him look older than he was. One of the kitchen women distributing the meals spoke pityingly to me one day: 'Alas, the poor old man, what a state he's in.' Another time, some women, probably watchers for other patients, came to me and asked what was my relationship to the patient. They could not decide if I was his wife, his daughter, or his daughter-in-law.

Two months passed in that way, meeting people and making friends. The one evening, I arrived in his room to find him covered with a kind of nettle-rash. Scratching madly, he told me that it had been so itchy the night before he had thought he would die. The more it itched, the more he scratched, wounding himself, tearing the skin off until he looked as if he had been burned. The pus had hardened into scabs and they were so painful they made him weep. The hospital explained that now the liver was improving and the toxins were coming out to the surface. But in such cases there were many fatalities, and there were constant whispered conferences. These were dangerous symptoms and the least mistake could be the last. They told me that the skin cells were dying.

But I did not wish to believe them, so I refused to believe them. His skin clung tightly to life. If it were cut or damaged it had always healed well, I knew. He once cracked the back of his head open, and after I had simply disinfected it, it had ached until the next day, then healed over. I felt sure that it would be the same this time too.

Doctor Chŏng, who was a surgical specialist, had a hard time: 'I don't know whether to believe you or the doctors.' A few days later he had a consultation with a skin specialist at the hospital and a treatment was begun.

He was washed all over, ointment was applied, and then he was wrapped in bandages so that if he shut his eyes he looked exactly like a mummy. He looked terrible.

When they were washing his skin it stung, he kept flinching and weeping: 'Ouch, ouch, oh God, forgive me, forgive me.' At a given moment a female internist was given charge of his treatment. We would undress him and support him while she disinfected his wounds and applied the medicine. As my husband stood there, stark naked, he kept up a steady stream of comments:

'You know, I'm really lucky.'

'Ah, why do you think you're lucky?'

'Just think how lucky I am to stand here naked and look at a pretty girl like you, ha ha ha.'

'Oh, is that so? Ho ho ho.'

'You're very pretty, very pretty.'

Laughing and crying in turns, he kept up the treatment but his condition only got worse. Every time the bandages sticking to his suppurating flesh had to be changed, the pain so bad that he screamed as though his last hour had come. At night he was hot and itching and sleep was slow to come; contemplating my husband once a light sleep had finally come to him, I would weep quietly.

I begged God to let him suffer less. That was all I asked. Every day a young preacher from Ch'unch'ŏn used to visit him; one day he called me outside. We sat at a street-side stall and ordered bowls of noodles; after a pause he spoke:

'I have no right to say anything, but don't you think

you have to prepare yourself for the worst? You have to take a firm hold of yourself.'

'Once everyone has done their utmost, if nothing works, there is nothing we can do about it, is there? Everyone is worrying and helping . . . now there's nothing to be done but leave it to fate whether he dies or not . . .'

'*Samonim,* if he dies, bury him here in Ch'unch'ŏn. There are lots of good spots around here.'

.'..Very well. If he should die now, he'd best be buried in Ch'unch'ŏn.'

Everybody seemed to be urging me to prepare myself. Sister Evelyn from Ireland had become a close friend of my husband's on her visits to the wards. One day she arrived with a priest and he administered the last rites. When she used to come, she and my husband would sing together, but on that day he lay there unable to speak.

Then one day he said that he wanted to see my mother. When I arrived with mother from Seoul he was so glad to see her that he cried bitterly. Mother too, seeing her son-in-law all wrapped in bandages and no doubt thinking that this was the last time they would meet, likewise wept without ceasing.

Mother stayed three days, then left for Seoul and when I returned to the hospital there were yet more tears.

'You've come, you've come; I thought I'd die without ever seeing you again.'

'Die? What do you mean, die?'

'It's alright now, now I've seen you it's alright, *kwench'ant'a.*'

Those two days were a critical moment, it seemed.

He spoke with an untypical, discouraged voice:

'God said I was to live to be eighty-eight before I died . . . he must have meant 1988! What do you think?'

'He told you to live to be eighty-eight, so why are you talking about 1988? You're not going to die. Why should you die?'

'You're right. I'm not going to die. He told me to live to be eighty-eight, so why should I die?'

Notwithstanding that he had always said God had told him he would live to the perfect age of eighty-eight, for those two days he was so discouraged that he began to wonder if God had not meant 1988.

All the time literary friends from Ch'unch'ŏn and Seoul as well as younger fans kept coming to make 'one last visit' and one particularly affected young man even began to make funeral laments outside the hospital's front door.

He remained in that state for some two weeks, then about one month after the crisis his scabs began to harden and fall off. Soon there was no further need to wrap him in bandages. A month before he left hospital the girth of his stomach had diminished considerably but he was nothing but skin and bones, so that we had to strap his wristwatch half way up his forearm. Because of his insistence on always wearing his watch, he had even worn it on top of the bandages too.

His scabs fell off, his stomach went in, but his belly-button stuck right out. Every morning, when the doctor came in on his rounds, my husband would ask him: 'Doctor Ku with your airs of an English gentleman!

Just when is this belly-button of mine going to go in?'

At which he would answer: 'Ah, just a little while longer and it will be alright. If you eat well it will be alright.' Doctor Ku was tall and handsome, and said very little, so my husband called him an 'English gentleman.'

About a week before he was to leave, his belly-button was still sticking out. One evening I reached the hospital to find him unable to speak for laughing.

'Only listen. Ha ha ha. I've laughed so much my belly-button will burst; I think I'll die.'

'What on earth is the matter?'

'Our English gentleman doctor came in on his visit this morning, so I asked him when this belly-button was going to fall off, and it was so funny, oh dear . . .'

The doctor's reply was a masterpiece:

'What, that belly-button? That is going to drop down and down, lower and lower, right down under the bed, and then it will fall off.'

He laughed and laughed, at the thought that such a sober person could say something like that.

'Doesn't the very thought of it make you laugh? Doesn't it make you laugh?'

It was nearing the end of May. The scabs had all fallen off, except for a few on his stomach and back where it was enough to apply ointment. He was getting better. One morning I got up early and was shocked on looking at the bed to see that one of his toe nails had come right off. Looking at his foot, I discovered that a new nail was growing in its place. All his toe nails and finger nails grew anew in the same way. The new nails that replaced the old ones were very delicate. He had sloughed off one complete skin.

On the day he went out of his sickroom for the first time after five months, he walked unaided for the first time. It was eight months since he had first fallen sick. He tottered on his own as far as the stairs, like a baby learning to take its first steps. Then Kwang-nae carried him down to the front door on his back and he tottered along on his own again, laughing out loud: 'I was several months in this hospital, it's wonderful!'

He was trembling with glee at the thought that this was the 'third miracle by which God had saved him.'

As low as low can be

# 'Lee Woi-su looks lonely'

Whenever the topic of his hospital bill came up, there was one question that he would always raise. Some time after he left hospital, he and his eccentric friends Chung Kwang the 'Mad Monk' and the long-haired novelist Lee Woi-su collaborated on a book of poems and paintings entitled 'The Three Bandits' and he kept on and on asking what became of his royalties.

'What the hell did you do with those six million Won?'

'When you were in hospital, you ran up a bill of over ten million Won. Do you think I can earn that amount with a tea-room? Besides, I have to repay the three million I borrowed to begin the business, and there's the deposit of one million as well; that makes four million already taken up.'

'Ah, really?'

A little while later he would repeat again, 'What the hell . . .'

'If you ask another time, I'll get angry. I already told you that four million are taken up in the cafe.'

'Ah, so you did.'

Sometimes he would insist that I had used up all his royalties from the book and call me a thief.

'You're the real thief!'

'I'm in charge of the 'Bandits' so how could I not be a thief too?'

He would giggle wildly: 'You thief, you! You're the real thief . . . We're just pure-hearted thieves.'

That was why I always kept the facts hidden from him. If a thousand copies had been sold, I used to tell him that five hundred had gone; while in fact they printed thirty thousand copies I would lie and tell him it was twenty thousand. If I told him the truth, he would have driven me mad asking day and night what I had done with all that money.

It had been Lee Woi-su's idea to produce the book, in order to help us, and he got Chung Kwang to agree to participate. My husband and Lee Woi-su first met in the hospital in Ch'unch'ŏn at the moment when his sickness was at its worst. Lee Woi-su came to visit him with his wife and two sons at the time when he was entirely wrapped in bandages, completely helpless, lying there like a mummy. He explained that he had liked Ch'ŏn Sang-pyŏng as a poet since he was in high school, but that he had never had an opportunity to meet him before until now he had come to visit.

My husband liked him at first sight too. He shouted out: 'Lee Woi-su, you're my little brother.' He must had heard about Lee Woi-su's style of living from some popular magazine or newspaper and somehow felt that they were similar. Hearing reports that he never washed for a week or a month on end, he explained that he thought: he's as eccentric as I am. He said that whenever he saw a photo of him, he had always been intrigued because he looked so very lonely.

'How odd; Lee Woi-su looks so sad.'

'Don't be so silly. He's got a pretty wife, two fine sons; what call has he to be sad?'

'That's right. Yet still, he looks really lonely.'

As soon as the family had left, he expressed his first impression: he was definitely lonely.

Then came the marijuana incident. When he saw in the newspapers that Lee Woi-su was involved in a group of marijuana users, he read the article several times, then started to pray. He asked God to forgive him. Somehow that lonely looking face kept coming into his mind and he explained that he had to pray instead of him.

'God, please forgive Lee Woi-su! Set him free quickly, please!'

After a moment of prayer, he proclaimed: 'God is sure to forgive him! He's sure to save him!' with great conviction, and began to chortle. Fortunately he was indeed soon released and the whole family came visiting nearly every day. Even though he was swathed in bandages and lying there quietly, as soon as they all came in he would shout aloud, calling out their names.

'Hanŏl! Jinŏl! You rascals!' he was inexpressibly fond of the two boys, who were already much taller than he was. The boys called him 'uncle' and when we went to visit their home in Ch'unch'ŏn later on, they called the money he gave them 'Precious Money' and refused to spend it, but instead kept it preciously mounted in a frame. They knew his poem '*Kwich'ŏn*' off by heart but if he asked 'Now, can you recite your uncle's poem?' they would politely reply, 'Only in our hearts.'

When the time came for him to be discharged, Lee Woi-su insisted that he should come and spend a few days resting in their home. I told him that we would get in touch but in the end we felt that we ought to go straight back to Seoul. It would not have been correct to bother them with an invalid and besides, my husband kept insisting that he 'wanted to see Ma quickly'.

Lee Woi-su waited to hear from us; finally he went up to the hospital and on finding the room empty he apparently went into such a rage that he had to be hospitalized on the spot, or so the tale goes. He was a terrible patient, a real trouble-maker, sneaking out to enjoy himself until all hours every evening.

Doctor Ku was dumbfounded: 'Ch'ŏn Sang-pyŏng used to do what he was told but this patient listens to nothing I say,' and in only a week he discharged him. In the years that followed, we would sometimes pay a visit to Lee Woi-su's house in Ch'unch'ŏn. There were always crowds of visitors, we used to stay awake all night with the whole family singing, playing the guitar, and laughing.

My husband used to complain: 'Lee Woi-su, why won't you wear your hair cut a bit shorter?' to which he would reply: 'If Chung Kwang the monk lets his hair grow long, I'll cut mine,' and we all rolled about clutching our stomachs and laughing.

# Divorce Papers

While he was in hospital, our financial situation was in a terrible state. On the day he went into hospital I took along five hundred thousand Won I had borrowed to be repaid in daily installments and when he left hospital I was still living on the same loan, which now amounted to two million Won. Even without counting his hospital bill, there were so many other expenses. Every week I was obliged to buy him two bottles of albumin at sixty-five thousand each, while bus fares, supper and snacks cost another thirty or forty thousand a day.

I had to endure other suffering at that time, too. When I had him admitted to hospital, people made heartless remarks: 'He's going to die anyway; why did she put him in hospital when their money is running out?,' 'Putting a dying man in hospital then borrowing money and running about on it; why, it's like selling a corpse.' Such words were daggers piercing my heart.

I could not so much as pay off the debt I had incurred on opening Kwich'ŏn, while people unaware of the fact went about whispering: 'She must be making a good living, why should she worry about the hospital bill?' Every time that kind of talk came up, I would say to the friends who shared my pain: 'I'm alright. I don't care what ignorant people say behind my back. They'll find out in due course. No one can say that I ran up debts that I asked them to repay, or that I claimed to be their close friend as I went running to them with my hand held out asking for help. If the interest is high, I'm the one using the money; if I take out daily-paid loans, I'm only keeping those people company, so I feel quite at ease. If an emergency arises, I can quickly go and borrow more; the interest rates may be high, but on the other hand, when I think about it I feel grateful.'

He was in hospital for a long time, the bill mounted up but thanks to Doctor Chŏng's help I was spared any great anxiety. I merely thought that I would repay the debt by going on running Kwich'ŏn until I died. When he emerged from the hospital, I was so happy I felt as if I was flying. I felt like shouting out: 'I saved my husband's life, I didn't go on about 'why put a dying man into hospital? and this and that'.'

It was when Lee Woi-su heard about how I was coping that he suggested publishing that book.

'*Samonim,* it's too hard for you. If you can find a publisher ready to advance you six million Won, sign a contract with them. You only have to select a few of Ch'ŏn Sang-pyŏng's poems, I can write novels and paint pictures, Chung Kwang *Sŭnim* has his things, let's the three of us do it together. I'll have a word with Chung Kwang.'

As a result 'The Three Bandits' was published and since I received all the money I really had become a thief.

I used the money to repay my debts and pay a deposit on the rent. I owed it all to the other two Bandits' kindness.

My husband and Chung Kwang *Sŭnim* were not able to meet very often but when they did, they made a great show of addressing each other affectionately with honorific titles: '*Posallim,*' '*Tosanim.*' The first time they met was when they were invited for a table-talk interview by a popular women's magazine. We went down to Kwangju, south-east of Seoul, where the Mad Monk was making pottery and as soon as my husband called him '*Posallim,*' Chung Kwang *Sŭnim* responded by calling him '*Tosanim,*' they both laughed merrily, and embarked on a *makkŏlli* party.

Chung Kwang explained that he had already met my husband in a photo. There was a picture of him that had been taken by Yun Myŏng-sik of Chungang University in the early 1970s, with a very particular atmosphere. He was leaning against a wall, his coat thrown over his shoulders, his eyes downcast, and Chung Kwang *Sŭnim* explained how amazed he had been at the sight of it.

'It was taken when you were utterly empty, completely without anything. I enquired who the man in the picture was and they told me it was the poet Ch'ŏn Sang-pyŏng. I wanted to meet you but never had the chance, so I made a drawing and put it away to give you when we met.'

He gave him a painting of a crane but while he was in hospital later, it passed into other hands on account of some unpaid debts. Chung Kwang was understanding: 'It's alright,' but regretfully explained, 'I would like to draw it again but my ideas when I drew it before were too simple, so the same drawing won't come out now.'

They could not meet very often but whenever Chung Kwang *Sŭnim* happened to drop in at Kwich'ŏn, my husband would always demand ten thousand Won in taxes from him. Hearing that he was worried about the cost of his mother-in-law's funeral, Chung Kwang reassured him: 'I'll make up whatever's lacking, so don't worry yourself about it.'

While he was in hospital, Chung Kwang came twice to visit him. Once he came by day and when I arrived that evening I was told, 'Chung Kwang *Sŭnim* called.' And that he had left a gift of two hundred thousand Won.

'Did you ever? Chung Kwang *Sŭnim* called, and he left two hundred thousand.'

'Really?'

'And do you know how he did it? I didn't realize it but after he was gone I put a hand under my pillow and there it was. That's the kind of person he is.'

The money in question was actually one hundred thousand Won that a doctor, who had been at the same school as my husband, had sent by way of Chung Kwang, with an extra hundred thousand that the Mad Monk had added. Gleeful as a child about this story, my husband even wrote a poem about it.

Yet it was on account of that two hundred thousand Won left by Chung Kwang that we ended up writing a divorce certificate. When that money came into his hands it seemed to him to be more than enough to feed and house him for the rest of his life. We had had cross words, so he pulled out the two hundred thousand, put it beside his pillow, and consulted with Kwang-nae.

'Kwang-nae, with that much we can go and live in a hotel, can't we?'

'Sure'

'Then let's you and I live together.'

'Sure'

'I've got two hundred thousand, so let's leave here, shall we, let's leave here.'

I had prevented him from smoking and he was vexed, so he was planning to live somewhere else with that two hundred thousand.

'Go on, go on. We'll divorce, if that's what you want. Divorce and get out, or not, do as you like. It'll spare me from any more trouble.'

'Alright, let's divorce, let's divorce.'

He seized hold of pen and paper and set about writing a divorce certificate.

At the top of the page he wrote 'Divorce Certificate' and below that 'To President Rho Tae-woo' then below that:

'Since my wife Mok Sun-ok keeps asking for a divorce I am writing this divorce certificate.'

When I asked him why he was writing to Rho Tae-woo, he replied, 'Because he's our President, that's why.'

In addition, the divorce was made out to be my wish, not his.

'Now do as you like. Here's your divorce certificate.'

'The two of us have to go to court and do it officially.

Just doing this is not enough.'

'I don't know anything about that. Do as you like, or not . . .'

'Put your thumbprint here.'

'I don't have to. You do it!'

He continued to refuse to put his thumbprint on the document, and the moment I enquired, 'Is it really alright for me to leave?' he gently subsided: '*Mundi Kashini*! How could you think of it?' and lowered his eyes. 'If you go, how could I go on living?'

He wrote an essay about 'Chung Kwang *Sŭnim* as I know him' in which he wrote:

> 'Whenever we meet, his simple appearance and his smile put me at ease. And when I look at his painting of a single crane hanging on the wall in Kwich'ŏn, I feel like turning into a crane and I long to go flying through the sky.
>
> 'Beside which, whenever I need some pocket money I only have to ask him and he gives it to me without hesitation. At the same time, he says, ' How happy you are to have met such an angel for a wife,' and so comforts my wife as well.
>
> 'Dressed in tattered rags, with a broken watch at his breast, and glittering baubles dangling from the hat on his head, he may look comic but no matter where he goes, no matter under what skies he swaggers, who could ever say anything against such an honest figure, with his smile as it is?
>
> '*Posallim*! Many thanks. Chung Kwang *Sŭnim*! We are brothers, always together.'

# Weeping at Brahms

I do not often cry. I tend not to let people see my tears, even when I am crying inside. Perhaps because I have a dry character, or because of all that I have endured in the course of history, the more I feel like crying the more I seem to have grown accustomed to bottling it all up inside myself.

Rather than encouraging open tears, the host of difficulties I encountered in looking after my husband only served to make me hide them more. If I was going to care for someone fragile as a baby and utterly childlike, as he was, I needed to be strong.

He was very different. He was such a frequent shedder of tears that he deserved to be given the nickname 'King of Tears.' If he heard some beautiful music, saw a fine painting, or just met a friend he was glad to see, tears would at once begin to flow silently from the corners of his melting eyes. If anyone wanted to see him cry, he was so fond of Brahms that they only needed to put on Brahms's Fourth Symphony and tears would readily flow in amazement that there could have been such a sensitive side to such an old man's heart.

My husband was fond of music, of classical music to be more precise, and there was never a day when he failed to listen to the FM radio classical music program. The radio was always kept tuned in to that channel and unless he went out he always listened to music.

KBS radio runs a program,
'Music You Hoped For'
every morning from five past nine until ten
and I never fail to listen to it.

Olympics of classical music! Festival.
I listen to the classical music program
because hope comes flowing from it:

I'm fond of Bach and Brahms,
today there was Bach but no Brahms,
so there'll be some Brahms tomorrow.

Once this poem was published in the morning edition of the *Hankuk Ilbo* and at once the KBS FM program put on some Brahms: 'In this morning's newspaper there was a poem by Ch'ŏn Sang-pyŏng, so . . .' We pricked up our ears at the commentary, then we heard the poem, followed by some music by Brahms. He was delighted: 'Oh! If that's the way to get them to play it, I must try again later on.'

He began to live surrounded by music when he was at university. While he was a refugee in Pusan, he mostly used to frequent a classical-music tea-room in the

Kwangbok-dong neighborhood, where he told me he became close friends with the artists Nam Kwan, Pak No-su, Kim Hwan-ki and others. Once back in Seoul, his favorite hideouts were the 'Dolce' and the 'Renaissance' music-rooms, in which you could sit in armchairs and listen to records of classical music for a small fee.

He admitted that from that time on, he would always weep copiously on hearing Brahms's Fourth Symphony. If I asked, 'But Beethoven is good too, why are you so fond of Brahms?' he would reply, 'Beethoven's tunes are too easy, Brahms's are more difficult, they touch me more.' Later he came to like Bach too, and he would say he felt that Brahms was like a voice from heaven, while Bach was like angels' voices.

At the sound of Brahms's Fourth the tears would flow at once. If I asked in mock amazement, 'But why do you cry when you hear good music?' he would simply murmur his nickname for me, '*Mundunga, Mundunga* . . .,' and keep on crying and snuffling. There was no record or cassette player at home, so whenever he came down to Kwich'ŏn I had to play that record for him and his expression would change as soon as it began.

Once after our marriage, in about 1983, we went to a music-room in Pusan called 'The Swan' in Kwangbok-dong. There we happened to meet a music-lover who had been close to my husband in his Pusan refugee period. He asked the girl in charge of the records to 'Please put on Brahms's Fourth Symphony for Ch'ŏn *Sŏnsaeng*.' The very moment that the music began to emerge from the speakers, my husband, who had until then been laughing noisily, abruptly burst into tears. He wept so intensely that the girl wept with him and his friend's eyes were moist with tears too.

When it came to singing, he was completely tone-deaf but if he had once heard a song he could remember the tune perfectly and he used to sing along. When he was listening to music, he was fully conversant with the name of the composer, the conductor, and even which movement this was, to such an extent that one felt he was like a music encyclopedia.

Among the commentators on the FM classical music channel he had many friends from the old days and sometimes, after hearing some commentator's remarks, he would grumble to me: '*Mundi Chashik*, he's simply repeating something I told him once, back in the old days.'

He loved Brahms very much, and there is one poem, 'Music,' in which he wrote about Brahms and his love for Clara Schumann:

> What kind of music is this? A quiet whisper close beside my pillow in the early hours. I think the composer of this tune, that I used to listen to with tears, loved one girl his whole life long. It may be that her name was Clara. Wasn't she his teacher's wife? One century, two centuries of time have rolled by and yet it looks as though his love is still not over. Early this morning it's come to the heart of this messed-up wreck living in a distant land and weeps.

## Tears in front of a painting

He invariably wept on hearing Brahms' Fourth, and likewise he wept at the sight of any painting that made him feel good. If there was a painting depicting a dilapidated house like ours, or a run-down neighborhood like the one we lived in, he would stand in front of it exclaiming, 'Wonderful!' and shedding copious tears.

He told me that he had been fond of painting since his school days, and that he had painted well himself. He used to get over ninety percent for drawing, and was an enthusiastic connoisseur as well. His art teacher had a book of reproductions of works of art that he borrowed briefly in his eagerness to see more paintings. Only it turned out that some of the paintings were so fine that he took a knife and cut them out. Fearing to be scolded, he said nothing when he returned the book, and he assured me that the teacher had not noticed.

'That's the kind of rogue I was. The mere sight of a good painting would drive me crazy . . .'

Naturally, therefore, whenever he came down to Insa-dong he used to make a pilgrimage of the art exhibitions in the galleries there. If he saw something he did not like, he used to swear as he walked out: 'You call that thing a painting? *Ssangnomui saekki*!'

Just as with poetry, he hated the abstract and the unintelligible. He loved paintings that had some universal aspect and that easily gave him feelings of peace. If he saw a painting he liked, he would want to buy it, but he always encountered my opposition: 'I've just seen a painting, it's wonderful, wonderful, marvelous, I need money to buy it. Get some money out of the bank.'

'What would you do with a painting if you had it? I can't let you have anything from our account.'

'Ssangnyŏnui kashina, Ssangnyŏnui kashina, you ignoramus, you're an ignoramus.'

Once he had vented his anger in that way he would soon calm down again, yet once he did finally get his painting. It was after his liver had been treated and he was back from hospital. He was having trouble with his joints, to the point that he was unable to walk so he had himself carried on piggyback to the Paeksŏng Gallery to look at some pictures. The artist whose work was on show was Park Sang-yun; he had come to Kwich'ŏn for a cup of quince tea and had urged us to 'come and visit my exhibition some time'.

Suddenly my husband began crying his eyes out in front of one particular watercolor. It showed a neighborhood with simple wooden houses, it felt just like the poor neighborhoods we used to frequent.

'Thank you, Lord! Thank you for letting me see such a wonderful picture! It's just like where we live. It's really wonderful!'

At the sight of my deeply moved husband crying so, Park Sang-yun and all the other visitors began to cry as well. Abruptly he turned to the artist: 'I'll buy it,' and held out his emergency fund of fifteen thousand Won as a down payment. 'I've got four hundred and twenty thousand in the bank; I'll go a draw that out for you, and what's left I'll pay off for the rest of my life.'

Once he had made the agreement all alone, he came and told me to get his four hundred and twenty thousand Won. Now that four hundred and twenty thousand Won was the Saemaŭl savings account I had opened in his name, paying in two or three thousand Won a day. Only since his discharge from hospital I had been obliged to withdraw three hundred thousand to use.

'No, it's not possible. Are we in any state now to buy paintings? It's not possible.'

'Not possible? Not possible? If you don't go and get that painting, I'll hold it against you until the day I die!'

He became very angry and ordered me to get the money, repeating: 'It costs several million, I'll repay what's left for the rest of my life.' He got Kwang-nae to carry him to the gallery and brought back two paintings, insisting that he was going to take them home with him. After reassuring him that I would bring them, they might get broken, I went to find the artist. I explained our real situation and told him he could sell the paintings to someone else. He replied: 'It's the first time I ever saw anyone so fond of my paintings that he cried. I'll let him have them, don't worry yourself about it; go and reassure him.'

When I reached home, I tried to calm him down but it was useless.

'Did you bring my paintings?'

'No I didn't'

'I kept telling you to look after them, and you haven't brought them?'

'What business do we have buying paintings in our situation? We have all those debts already, how could you strike that bargain? You didn't even ask me.'

*'Ssangnyŏnŭi kashina, Ssangnyŏnŭi kashina,* you ignoramus, you're an ignoramus. Those pictures are so good, I want to keep looking at them all the time until I die, and you're preventing me! You're preventing me! Ignoramus! I'll hold it against you until the day I die. *Ssangnyŏnui kashina!*

'I don't have that money now! We have so many debts, there's no money to give him. In our situation, do you realize what a huge sum five hundred thousand Won is?'

'You ignoramus, ignoramus, *Ssangnyŏnui kashina.*'

The day after our argument, on learning that the artist was giving him the pictures, he was so content that he couldn't stop talking: 'How wonderful, just like our neighborhood, isn't it?'

I felt too embarrassed simply to take them and determined to get together at least five hundred thousand Won to pay for them. Some people happened to hear about it all, exclaimed, '*Aihyu,* if he's that fond of them, we'll help a bit . . .' and they set up a collection box.

However, the collection idea fell through, on account

of the artist's polite refusal to accept any payment. For his exhibition the following year Yŏng-jin made him a traditional light summer costume, and that was the only way we were able to express our grateful feelings.

My husband hung one of the paintings in Kwich'ŏn and one at home and used to go into ecstasies every time he saw them. Later, Kim Yŏng-ja held an exhibition at the same gallery. My husband liked his work and used to tell visitors to Kwich'ŏn, 'Let's go and see, there are some fine paintings!' and drag them off.

'Better than Picasso! Better than Rodin! Don't you want to go and see the paintings?'

Limping along, he would go daily to look and look again at the paintings he liked. On another visit to a gallery, he phoned me: There was a really wonderful painting, I was to go and draw out five hundred thousand Won. It was a work by Ch'oi Ul-ga and since I finally bowed to my husband's insistence, the painting now hangs at home.

'Just you try to sell those two paintings. I'll divorce you.'

'Ok, let's sell the paintings and get a divorce!'

'*Mundunga! Mundunga! Aigu, Mundunga*!'

Those paintings, that he had got after begging, threatening, fighting, and defeating his wife, were like victory trophies to him.

On a later occasion he wrote an essay entitled 'An Artist I Know' in which he explained that there was an artist he had been close friends with since his refugee days in Pusan, Nam Kwan *Sŏnsaeng-nim*, but that he could not for the life of him recall how they had first met.

He went on, 'I long to own one of my dear friend Nam *Sŏnsaeng*'s pictures but with my poor pockets, it's a dream beyond my hopes. I will just have to be content with knowing Nam Kwan himself,' in resigned tones.

The artist he was closest of all to was Ha In-du, who died of cancer a few years ago. He was very close, my brother's friend as well as my husband's close companion, so that he used to consider me as a real brother would.

Their companionship dated from my husband's second year of university, spent in Pusan, and from that time onward they were very close: 'I don't need to use any kind of formal terms with him. If I address him formally, it sticks in my throat, I start to laugh, and all that comes out is a fart. I recently heard from my wife that he was in hospital. She was very worried for him.'

I had been so worried I was crying and he had shouted at me:

'*Mundunga,* old In-du's not going to die yet. God isn't calling him home yet, you know . . .. You're just ignorant, you don't know. What are you crying for?' He kept shouting again and again. 'In-duya, *Yonoma,* get up! I'll soon be up again too. Don't you realize that someone like you has no right to go up to be with God yet . . .?'

Yet soon after one last exhibition of paintings incorporating poems, Ha In-du died. And now my husband has gone to heaven too, so I can't help but wonder if he, my brother, and Ha In-du are not sitting up there enjoying a drink together.

## Every pretty girl his sweetheart

Ch'ŏn Sang-pyŏng had any number of sweethearts. If a woman appealed to him, there was no asking her how she felt about him, she was chosen to be one of his sweethearts on the spot. If a pretty girl happened to pass by as he walked down the street or sat in a car, he would stare at her piercingly. Any ordinary person would have glanced furtively once for just a moment, but he used to scrutinize her thoroughly for as long as he pleased.

When there was some girl that he was inspecting intently, I would ask him: 'Have you chosen another secret sweetheart?' and he would reply: 'That's right.' He loved 'pretty' girls. It made no difference whether it was her face, her hand, or her foot that was pretty. He had only to catch sight of a pretty girl to get carried away and start humming.

A 'secret sweetheart' was one that only needed to be stored away in his heart, nothing more; as a result, if he saw a pretty girl he freely chose her for a sweetheart. He met many of these secret sweethearts at Kwich'ŏn. If a girl with a pretty face came in, he would admire her, murmuring: 'Pretty face, pretty face.' If she came in with someone else, he might mutter: 'Very pretty hands, very pretty hands.' If he remarked on the pretty hands, he meant that the face was not pretty.

'My sweetheart, my sweetheart.'

If a girl pleased him, he would make his pledge to her, hold her hand, keep company with her. A certain Mrs. No, who wrote poems, was already a mother of children but he still spoke to her in familiar tones and called her his sweetheart. If she appeared he would address her fondly: 'Why have you been away so long? Why have you been away so long?'

Before her poems were approved and she was recognized as a poet, they went together to Myŏngdong Cathedral and he prayed in front of the statue of the Virgin Mary: 'Maria-*nim,* please let Mrs. No's poems be approved.' They even went hand in hand like children to Kyŏngbok-kung Palace and had their photo taken, provoking the envy of the other sweethearts.

Still, even after he had sworn several times that someone was his sweetheart, if he did not see her for a few months he frequently forgot her completely. He would chose some other girl as his sweetheart instead. If he managed to switch sweethearts in this way, like eating cold porridge, without ever getting himself sworn at, it was because his heart was as clear as a flowing stream and he was utterly selfless.

'*Sŏnsaeng-nim,* I thought that back before you told me I was your sweetheart but now you can't even remember my name? I won't be your sweetheart any more.'

Sometimes his former sweethearts would speak like

that, and he would explain: 'I forget all sorts of things. I even forget my own name.' But at other times he would snap back: 'I never chose you for my sweetheart!' It was not something he did deliberately. Simply there were times when things went blank and he could not recognize people in the slightest. Sometimes a phone call would come from someone he found hard to remember, and he would hang up with a hasty, 'Um . . . um . . . Look, I must go and have a pee, I can't talk now.' The caller might know him perfectly well, he was sure it was someone he did not know.

There was a Mrs. Song he had been very close to in his youth but she had been living in the States for many years; she had seen him only a few years before but when she met him the next time he had no memory of her at all.

'*Sŏnsaeng-nim,* don't you remember? How last time in Kwanghwa-mun you asked me to marry you?'

'When did I do such a thing? I never did.'

She was upset, and sent a lengthy letter full of memorable episodes and talk of the family, intended to stir his memory. She asked me to add additional details in an attempt to help him recall after he had read the letter, so I added other stories of the old days and asked him if now he remembered, but still he insisted that he knew nothing of her. In the end it seemed that the blanks were partial; there were things he remembered vividly and others that had vanished completely.

Even forty years after the event, the memory of his first love still remained vivid in his mind. While he was a refugee at Pusan in his second year of university, he was so eager to see a girl named Pyŏn In-ho from the humanities college that he even audited language classes she was taking. When she appeared, he would be so overjoyed he would tell her frankly how his heart was beating wildly, like an adolescent boy confessing his love.

According to the dramatist Shin Bong-sŭng, who was his close friend, once down in Pusan when there was no sign of her Ch'ŏn Sang-pyŏng enquired and was told that she had gone on some business to the island of Yŏng-do. He accordingly went to the street leading from the bridge linking Yŏng-do with the city and waited all day long for her to come back; just as night was falling, he noticed a bus speeding past and uttered a 'damn.' It had not struck him before that she might go speeding past in a bus, not because he was stupid, but because he was so absorbed and so innocent.

He related that the affair had come to an end a year later, when the girl left to study in America.

'Poor dear, unrequited love . . . what a sweetheart to have.'

'Not at all, not unrequited, it wasn't unrequited. She said she liked me.'

'How much did she like you?'

'I was never once able to hold her hand.'

'Did you talk about marriage?'

'She suggested we go to America together but how could I ever go to America? So we parted. There was no one after that. Now there's only you.'

From time to time old loves would come to mind, but he would always insist that he loved me best of all.

# Poor naked Simon, so deep and warm

His behavior became like that of a child once he developed his cirrhosis of the liver. After he had been taking liver medicine for a long time he began to manifest nervous and mental symptoms because of the side effects. From about a week before he was due to leave hospital, his spirits were in such a state of excitement that he was unable to sleep for even one hour a night. It seems that if someone takes medicine to treat a liver condition for too long, they go into a kind of coma, and his state was a variety of that. He could not sleep a wink, his eyes glittered brightly, he was never at a loss for words, they flowed effortlessly. During the day he might shut his eyes for ten minutes or so, but otherwise he never slept.

'*Ŏmma-yo,* I'm back. I've come back alive. *Ahyu,* how fine our house is, how fine . . . I was so anxious to see you, I nearly died.'

Returning home after his release from hospital, he was relaxed and happy, and still he did not sleep. The following day it was the same. He did not sleep but kept talking about the old days, although his memory was not very good. He wrote poems too, including some in Japanese. He seemed in a quite new kind of mood, as if he felt he had returned to the days of his youth.

The friend who had sent money through Chung Kwang *Sŭnim* was a doctor who had specialized in psychiatry, Chŏn Mun-ui, and a few days later I took him to her clinic. After he took some medicine, he became much calmer but he was nonetheless another man. His eyes continued to sparkle brightly, he never felt inclined to sleep, and he would fly into a rage at the least contradiction.

He suddenly screamed at Kwang-nae: '*Ssangnomui saekki*, I can't stand the sight of you. Get out!' Or he would be sitting in Kwich'ŏn when he would abruptly get angry for no reason: 'I want to go somewhere else!' and would go roaming the tea-rooms or art-galleries. He kept taking the medicine and gradually got better.

After about a month, he began to leave the house increasingly frequently with no thought or preparation. Having told us that he was not going out, he would slip on a pair of rubber slippers and catch a bus to go down to the city centre just as he was, wearing his indoor clothes.

If he meant to come to Kwich'ŏn, he used to get off the bus and then he had to cross the road over a foot-bridge. He clambered up and down the steps holding on to the railings, which left his hands as black as if he had been delivering coal briquettes; then he would keep rubbing his face with those hands until it was a perfect mess, smothered in sooty stains.

Midway along there was the Crown Bakery cake-shop; since the weather was warm, he used to call in there and eat a bowl of flavoured ice-shavings. There the girls serving, who knew him, would wipe off his face and hands. Once he had finished eating, he would be sure to insist: 'Let's hold hands, let's hold hands,' and if they had not seen him for a few days the kind girls used to worry and ask me, 'Why don't we see *Sŏnsaeng-nim* around nowadays?'

From the cake-shop, Kwich'ŏn is about five hundred yards down the road; he used to stop and sit down to rest his aching legs several times along the way. He would come staggering in, quite unaware of the mess his face would be in again; then I would wash him and tidy him up.

'You told *Ŏmma* before you came out, didn't you? You know how much we worry when you just leave like that!'

'Well, you see . . . I just walked out and somehow, without realizing it, I got on the number 20 bus, you see! That's how it happens, it can't be helped.'

'What did you do about the bus fare?'

'I got a twenty Won reduction! 'I'm sorry,' I said, 'I don't have any more money' and gave him two hundred Won. The drivers all know I don't have any money, they look after me.'

He used to enjoy taking the bus most of all. Then he could read all the shopsigns along the roadside. In order to see them clearly, he had to sit in the very front seat on the other side to the driver. He used to see he hated the subway because it ran under the ground and you could see nothing outside. As he studied the signs, if he spotted any mistake he would swear.

'Those *ssangnomŭi saekki*! Those ignoramuses! Look what they've written there.'

From the time he got on until he got off, he would all the time be reading the shopsigns along the street, swearing and muttering to himself. He continued to take the medicine and his mental confusion slowly disappeared, but for several years he had to keep on taking the liver medicine as well as his tranquilizers, and a tonic. Fortunately his stomach was strong and although he had to take several different kinds of medicine for such a long period, it never made him ill and generally speaking he remained in good health.

Once he began to grow a little bit stronger, he started to drink small amounts of liquor; at first I used to allow him just two glasses of beer a day. Also I began to give him two thousand Won as pocket-money each day. He would buy icecream with it, or share it out in gifts among his tiny friends in the neighborhood. Once his physical and mental problems were over, he looked truly happy again.

I'm the happiest man
in the world.

Since my wife runs a café
I've no need to worry about making ends meet
and I went to university
so there's nothing lacking in my education
and because I'm a poet

my desire for fame is satisfied
I have a pretty wife too
so I don't think about women
and we have no children
no need to worry about the future
we have a house as well
I'm really very comfortable.
I'm fond of *makkŏlli*
my wife always buys it for me
so what have I got to complain of?
Besides
I firmly believe in God
and since the mightiest person
in the whole wide world
is looking after my interests
how can anyone say misfortune's coming?
('Happiness')

Anyone who is contented with the world he is in is happy. He was contented with the world he found around him. Or rather he demanded that the people around him make him feel contented with the world, and trained them accordingly. Perhaps I should say that he used to do exactly as he liked, and freely trained the people around him to approve his way of living and adjust to it. He never bothered in the slightest about how any one else felt, but spoke as he wished and acted as he felt inclined to.

If there was someone he felt fond of, he would phone them at the crack of dawn and go dashing off to visit them. He was famous for that from youthful times. The poet An Chang-hyŏn, who was famous for his incessant demands that Korean literature should use only the Korean alphabet, was very close to my husband. When my husband felt like seeing him, he would go straight over, in the middle of the night.

'I'm going to see old Chang-hyŏn!'

If he ever woke up and the thought came to his mind, he would be off just like that. When he got there, if he could not find the proper apartment block, he would wander about shouting, 'An Chang-hyŏn! An Chang-hyŏn!' with whatever voice he could produce. Once all the people in the block had been properly woken up, An Chang-hyŏn would reconize Ch'ŏn Sang-pyŏng's voice and go hurrying out to find him.

It was the same with the telephone. If he had anything to discuss with the people he liked best, he usually phoned them at early dawn. When it came to people like the writer Han Mu-suk, the poets Kim Nam-jo or Ku Sang, if he wanted to see them he would phone, skip the opening formalities, and get straight to the point: '*Sŏn-saeng-nim*, it's Ch'ŏn Sang-pyŏng! Let's get together today, yesyesyes,' and then he would hang up, with no way of knowing if that person had agreed to meet him that day, or what.

Once he made an appointment to meet Han Mu-suk after not seeing her for a long time. She arrived at Kwich'ŏn with her son and his wife, as well as her husband's friend Ko Kwang-su. It was a Sunday and there were a lot of customers, so I suggested they go and have lunch first. Soon after, my husband came in alone.

'Why have you come back alone?'

'Because I've finished my lunch.'

'For goodness' sake, how can anyone act like that? You haven't seen them for ages; you should talk, then come back here all together. Why did you come out?'

'I wanted a pee, that's all.'

'First you make them all come out, then you gobble up your food first and come out alone . . . really!'

'*Kwench'ant'a, kwench'ant'a, kwench'ant'a,* I wanted a pee, that's all.'

He never gave so much as a thought as to what others might feel. I had more than a few embarrassments on account of his not being able to see the other person's point of view. There was a frequent customer at Kwich'ŏn, commonly known as Chairman Mo, who was very fond of my husband. He had a big foreign car and I felt very sorry because my husband used to enjoy using it to have himself driven to town and back.

At seven in the morning he would phone him: 'Mo Kyŏng-guk *Ssi*! I want you to drive me! Down to Kwich'ŏn, the time to drink a cup of tea, then back home before two.'

Once he had outlined his schedule, he would hang up without more ado. Asking him to come up to our house, drive him down to Kwich'ŏn, wait for him, then drive him back home; his driver's day was ruined but he never showed any hint of being embarrassed. He had no sense of such things. Every week he would phone like that two or three times, until I finally erased the number; but he had memorized it and continued to call.

'Chairman Mo, my husband's like that, so you must tell him you're busy. I even rubbed out your telephone number from the book.'

'Don't think of it like that, *Samonim*. I drive him when I have nothing to do, so don't worry. It gives me exercise.'

Thanks to his patience, my husband was able to travel in luxury for a few months but I used to stop him from grabbing the telephone and bothering people every day and slowly it grew rarer. He was so immersed in his own affairs and thoughts that he frequently had no idea who was there beside him. If we were to go out together in the morning, he would go out into the garden first and stand there motionless. I would call out:

'You go on ahead. I'll follow you in a minute; you go on up to the bus stop and wait.'

I would repeat the same thing several times but he would go on standing there as if he had not heard.

'Aren't you coming? Aren't you coming?' he would ask, completely taken by the idea that we were going to walk up together when I came out. Or we would be walking up together when he would suddenly stop: 'I must have a pee.'

'You should have gone before we set out; why wait till now?'

'Because I want to go now, that's all.'

'What will the neighbors think if they see?'

'Nobody's looking, nobody's looking.'

'They're looking. They can all see as they go by.'

'I'm having a pee, what business have they looking? I don't look at them, why should they look at me?'

Mention of that story reminds me of another. He had come down to Kwich'ŏn one Friday and was on his way home alone. Near the East Gate bus stop he felt a suddenly need to urinate. He went into a nearby coffee-shop, relieved himself, and on his way out said to the woman in charge: 'A naval lieutenant will be coming along soon. Just tell him to wait, his friend will be back in a little while.' He told me the story when I came home that evening. 'But why on earth a naval lieutenant?' I asked him. '*Mundunga,* because army lieutenants are so common, silly.'

There was no telling where such sudden flashes of wit came from. Sometimes I even wondered if he wasn't just pretending. But it was simply a moment of wit that came, then vanished again.

He was so thoroughly immersed in his own thoughts, he knew exactly his own likes and dislikes; he was unlike other people in his evaluation of what mattered or not. Fans would often come visiting at home. The initial welcome was equally cordial for them all, but after talking for a while, if he did not take to someone he made no further effort. 'I'm not feeling very well. I must get some sleep,' he would say, lying down with his face to the wall, and closing his eyes.

Once a particular visitor came to Kwich'ŏn. He made a great bow to my husband, took him out and bought him a glass of beer, then they came back. Perhaps he was drunk; at any rate, he began to talk utter nonsense. My husband could not stand rowdy drunks, so he made no reply. No matter what he said, he simply sat there, his eyes closed, not speaking a word. After a little while, he suddenly spoke up: 'I say, there's a good place near here. I'll take you there, let's go,' and began to lead the way outside. I was afraid he would drink more liquor and tried to restrain him: 'You mustn't drink any more.'

He smiled and whispered in my ear: 'Don't worry! I'll just dump him there and come back.' I don't know how he managed it, but he left the other fellow there and soon reappeared. From then on, if that man came in sober he would talk freely with him, but if he came after drinking he would refuse to utter a single word.

Readers would sometimes phone, but after a moment's conversation, if the caller was talking nonsense he would interrupt: 'I must go and have a pee,' and hang up.

Just as his likes and dislikes were clearly defined, so too there was a very big difference between the way he treated things he considered important and those he did not. Things that mattered to him he would keep checking, discussing them over and over again, while things he thought to be insignificant he did not bother his mind about.

He paid absolutely no attention to things like the date when an article was due, so I had to look after that. Reporters who did not know him very well would take seriously his 'Yes, yes,' to their request, and wait quietly until the deadline was past.

'I don't know, is that what I said? I've forgotten.'

Even if he was asked to write something, he made no memo, and did not remember either. The only thing that counted for him was to say that he would write something, he saw no sense in the idea that it had to be written by such and such a date.

He attached immense importance to matters of daily life that we consider insignificant, like when he had to be shaved or when a light bulb had to be changed. One evening I suggested shaving him. He firmly replied: 'Get me up tomorrow morning at seven thirty and shave me at seven forty.' The next morning I was busy and let the time pass, until I was suddenly scolded: 'Aren't you going to give me a shave?'

'I'll do it tonight.'

'Evenings are no good! Shave me now, shave me now!'

'Oh dear, what can I do? I forgot to buy a razor-blade.'

'You forgot to buy one! You forgot that? How could you forget that again?'

'You must phone me. If you phone me I'll remember.'

He did not forget, and a call duly came through to Kwich'ŏn.

'Did you buy it?'

'I'll go out and buy it in a little while.'

'You could shut the door for a minute, surely.'

I knew he would go on phoning until I told him I'd bought it, so I would lie brazenly.

'Oh yes, of course, I already bought it. I bought it but then I forgot. I'll bring it with me later on.'

He would switch the elctric light on and off even during the daytime, so he was extraordinarily concerned about the bulbs.

'Something terrible's happened, something terrible!'

'What's the matter?'

'That bulb. If you leave it on it will burn itself out after a month or so.'

'If it burns out, I'll just have to change it. I've got several in reserve, so why are you worrying?'

'Do you know how to change a light bulb?'

'Of course I know.'

'I reckon you're not tall enough.'

'What do you mean, not tall enough?'

'Stand up and try, go on.'

'Look, I can reach it easily.'

'Ah, right, so you can, so you can.'

If something seemed important to him, he could only set his mind to rest by continually checking that it was alright. Things he liked he performed without hesitation, important things he kept on and on checking. It may be because of the way in which he kept checking and pondering about things that to our eyes seem insignificant that he came to be considered an eccentric.

# *Mundunga,* my love

'*Aneya*! Wife!'

That was what he used to call me when he was in a really good mood. That rarely-heard word was full of the most unimaginable tenderness. He used a lot of names to address me by: *Aneya,* meaning wife; *Okiya* and *Sunoka,* my name; *Mundunga,* meaning leper; *Manura,* implying old woman; *Komoya,* meaning aunt; and *Mundi Kashina,* meaning leper's daughter. I could detect how he was feeling at any given moment by the name he chose to address me by. When he was happy, he would smilingly call me '*Mundunga, Mundunga*' and, although it may not seem so very different, when he was in quite the opposite mood he would use '*Mundi Kashina*', usually closely complemented with an oath: '*ssangnyŏn*'. Even when he used the same '*Mundi*' or '*Mundunga*' the tone could vary in subtle ways.

Once my mother was sitting with us and he kept calling me '*Mundi Kashina*' until at last she interrupted: 'In that case, am I supposed to be the leper? I'm the leper and she's my daughter, isn't that why you keep calling her leper's daughter?' To which he replied in a flash: 'Why no, she's the leper; I would never call you names like that, *Ŏmma.*' Whenever Mother put on a serious expression, he would immediately employ guile and give a display of quick-wittedness.

The worst insult he was capable of, although he never used it against me, was, 'You frog-like female.' I don't really know, but I think he meant the imprecation to suggest the feeling of a frog's fickleness and imprudence. After our marriage, the first time I was frequently cursed was when I was running the old furniture store in Hwanghak-dong. If I shut up shop at five and got home by six or at the latest seven, I heard no oaths. If I was any later, oaths came pouring out, as he demanded to know where I had been, whom I had met, what rascal I had been with.

'I was just coming out when a customer showed up; the time to drink a cup of tea and talk, and I was late. Why? Don't you want me to go out any more?'

'How can you not go out? But in future just make sure you're home by six or seven.'

Usually that would be an end of it. I knew that he was interrogating me suspiciously in that way because he loved me, so I just ignored the oaths. But once it was worse.

'Why are you so late? *Ssangnyŏnŭi kashina,* who have you been coming on with?'

'What did you say? Really, there's nothing you won't say. Right, I'm leaving.'

As I stormed out in anger, I reflected that I would have to make him change his attitude. So I went home to

Mother. I walked for about fifteen minutes over rough unmade-up paths although it was gone eleven, and gave Mother a tremendous shock. I explained that I wanted to change his habits and the two of us put our heads together.

In those days little Yŏng-jin was attending primary school and she would invariably drop in at our room on the way to school. The next morning I sent her to tell her uncle to come and have breakfast at their house; then I went down to the town. Yŏng-jin duly went and seems to have put on quite a performance.

When she enquired, 'Where's aunty gone?' my husband could make no reply and when he came for breakfast at mother's he was seriously worried. A little later I went to where he was sitting as usual in the Yuchŏn tea-room and sat down opposite him; he looked delighted.

'How did you know I'd be here?'

'Don't you ever say things like that again.'

'Where did you go yesterday?'

'Where do you think I went? To Mother's of course. She told me to come back home if it was like that.'

'How did you get there so late? You're always afraid.'

'If you're angry enough you stop being afraid.'

'But Yŏng-jin, well, what a kid. Where's auntie gone? she asked. She's not come back, I said. Well, what a kid, just she wait . . .'

After that he never used such harsh language again. If he ever started to ask, 'Where have you been? What rascal did you meet?' I would reply, 'Shall I do it again?'

and he would hold his peace. So I stealthily corrected his way of speaking.

'When I'm upset, I'm capable of saying anything. It's when you're late, I get worried, that's why.'

In actual fact we never had a real fight. There has to be a serious, two-sided conflict for there to be a fight and we were never in conflict. He could swear blue murder and shout his head off, but all that was mere hot air. If we both got angry, he would 'turn into a loach again' as he put it in a poem. He used to calm down in a flash, rather as a little child that has been pestering its mother falls silent at once when she finally shouts.

He used to get angry about nothing. Since he was sensitive and warm-tempered, he was always apt to throw a tantrum. One moment it would be a good-tempered '*Mundunga, mundunga,*' and a second later some trifle would turn it into an angry, '*Ssangnyŏna*!' One moment he would be agreeing, 'Yes, right,' then there would be a sudden switch to, 'I won't, I won't, I won't!'

I used to joke about him being a living example of capriciousness. In order to overcome it, I had to act in an equally capricious way.

'You ignoramus! *Ssangnyŏnŭi Kashina*!'

'Why are you taking so angrily? Do you want me to start?'

'What do you mean, you start? You think I'm trying to win? *Ssangnyŏnŭi Kashina*! Ignoramus!'

'Of course I'm ignorant. How come an intelligent person is so good at swearing? Suppose I call you a *ssangnomŭi saekki* every time you call me *ssangnyŏn*?

Who will be the worse for that?'

Whenever I gave the impression I was getting really angry, he would stop his cursing and do a complete turn-about. He would merely blink repeatedly, grumble to himself, and say nothing more. At such moments I could hear in my heart what was happening inside him, just like the fluttering heart-beats of baby sparrows you feel when you take them between your hands. He was sorry for having troubled me. A few moments later, I would have to comfort him, stroking his hair or pulling the quilt up over him.

'*Aigu,* what a character . . . Don't you wonder what you'd do without me? . . .. What a temperament you've got, making me angry like that . . .'

He would stay silent, looking utterly desolate, and I would start to talk wildly about this and that. 'I say, do you remember that Mr. Kim . . .?' I would bring the conversation to a point where he would begin to nod his head.

I was told of a certain professor who once asked a journalist who had come to interview him about my husband. He remarked: 'It's a shame about Mok *Yŏsa.* How can she go on living with someone like that? She's a talented woman, surely she's wasted on someone like Ch'ŏn Sang-pyŏng?' He felt so sorry for me, he went so far as to ask if he didn't think I ought to get a divorce and live happily.

Then one day it appears that the professor happened to meet my husband. From that moment, he could be heard declaring: 'Having met Ch'ŏn Sang-pyŏng, I can tell you, he'd be lost without Mok *Yŏsa*' and explaining that he had been mistaken in his previous opinion. 'He's innocent as a baby, but with a character like that, there's no one but her could ever put up with him.' He began regularly to ask after my husband, too.

Strangers used to remark to me that I was an odd sort of person. Just like that professor at the beginning, they wondered how we were living as husband and wife. As man and woman, that is. In that sense, of course, the immediate reply was, 'Not at all.' I could never think of him as husband; I lived by the thought that if I did not look after him, he could not live.

My husband was like a child. He was fragile, too wounded to be able to fight. He could not even imagine me vanishing from his side. I suppose that people used to consider me odd because I was prepared to live as someone so absolutely needed.

For about a fortnight before our wedding we lived together in our rented room, but he never once so much as held my hand. When the wedding ceremony was over, he pronounced in solemn tones: 'Now we are husband and wife.' He even went so far as to declare solemnly that on that date we would take the appropriate action but in reality, nothing changed for us.

He always used to say: 'If the people at the security agency had only given me electric shock torture twice, we could have had children, but they did it a third time, so we couldn't.' We had no choice but to be husband and wife without any 'sex'.

I remember something that happened while we were living in that lodging house in Sanggye-dong with the twelve families. One morning when I went out into the yard, all the young wives began to cackle with laughter.

'Hey, why were you talking like that yesterday evening?'

'What? What were we saying?'

'*Hee hee hee. Aigu,* your old man, the way he kept saying, 'Let go, let go, let go!'

The rooms in the house were one next to another, and it was an old building so that at night every word could be heard. Only they were claiming that sounds of love-making had come from our room the night before.

'What was it like?'

'You say he doesn't like it, so why were you touching him? Ha ha ha.'

'*Ayu,* It's different when you're young.'

Actually, when it was time to sleep, we had spread one eiderdown over the two of us, but later we had each tried to pull it more to our own side and they had misunderstood the sense of his repeated, 'Let go!' In the night he had twisted and kicked until he had pulled the eiderdown entirely to his side and I had nothing left to cover myself with. Therefore I had started to pull at the eiderdown and he, determined not to be robbed, had shouted out his cries of 'Let go.'

'When you were pulling at the eiderdown, we thought you were holding on to your husband's whatsit,' they all giggled.

People may not be able to understand, but an expression I used to like to hear was *Ch'ŏnsaeng-yŏnpun* 'A union ordained by Heaven.' I had a friend who told fortunes and made horoscopes. When she compared our horoscopes, she exclaimed: 'Why, you and Ch'ŏn *Sŏnsaeng-nim*'s is a union ordained by Heaven!' My husband kept that expression engraved in his heart and used to bring it out at the least provocation.

'Go on, get a divorce. I don't mind!'

'Why, do you think you could ever find another husband?'

'Of course I can.'

'You're too old, how could you ever . . .?'

'Do you want to see me try?'

'*Ssangnyŏnŭi kashina*, what would happen to me? At my age, what would I do? I could never find another wife.'

'But I could find a new husband!'

'*Mundi Kashina*, who would ever want an old woman like you?'

'Do you want to see?'

He would remain silent.

'How can I, if I've got you?'

'*Mundunga*, you and I are *Ch'ŏnsaeng-yŏnpun*, so how can you? That's what your friend told you, isn't it? *Ch'ŏnsaeng-yŏnpun* . . .'

*Ch'ŏnsaeng-yŏnpun*: having said farewell to the husband I spent twenty-two years with, I reckon I know the full meaning of that expression. There are times when I suddenly sense very clearly that it was on account of all those feelings we two shared that other people could not know; the affection we two shared that other people did not bother to try to understand; the private moments shared by just the two of us, that other people would find hard to imitate. It was because there were those things that we were able to spend a lifetime together, and I feel sure that is what 'a destiny united in the heavens' means.

Like everybody else, we had our own special ways of expressing affection. Occasionally, and it really was only occasionally, he would suddenly squeeze my hand until it hurt. That was his own special way of touching my heart, just as he had his own special way of writing poems. His way of squeezing my hand without saying anything when I was looking particularly loveable, or pretty, was a gesture expressing fully the immense care for me he had in his heart. Capricious and obstinate though he might seem, he had his own coy, private means of expression.

Once I had gone across to the room where I slept, I would feel his gaze come flying and fixing on my face through the glass in the door; if I turned to look in his direction, there would be his eyes locked with mine. At such moments, bashfully, he would close his eyes firmly. A little later, if our eyes met again as his searched for mine, I would lift a hand and pretend to give him a little slap; whereupon he would lift his hand in return, as if to say 'Ouch!'.

The first of all the women I like
can only be my wife
of course.

(From: 'The women I like')

He wrote that poem as a confession that he liked me most of all, while I used to keep asking him about our relationship and he would gladly reply.

'You're grateful to your *manura,* aren't you? Really grateful?'

'Thank you dear, thank you, thank you. It's entirely thanks to you that I'm alive.'

'Do you love your *manura*?'

'Of course I love you, of course.'

'So who do you love most?'

'I love my wife best of all.'

'Did you always love me? From the very start?'

'Of course I did. From the very beginning, deep inside, I loved you.'

When he used to tell me that he had loved me even before our marriage, he always insisted that I respond: 'So tell me it was the same for you, tell me you felt the same.'

'Of course I did. *Sŏnsaeng-nim,* you're the only one, who else could there be? I tell everybody. I loved you from ever such a long time ago. I still love you, now that you've gone back to heaven. You must treasure me and only me in your heart up there until the time comes for me to follow you. Once we're together up there, I don't expect there will be anybody pointing at us and saying, 'What an odd couple' any more.'

If he can hear my promise up there in heaven, I'm sure he must be calling out affectionately: '*Mundunga, mundunga, mundunga*!'

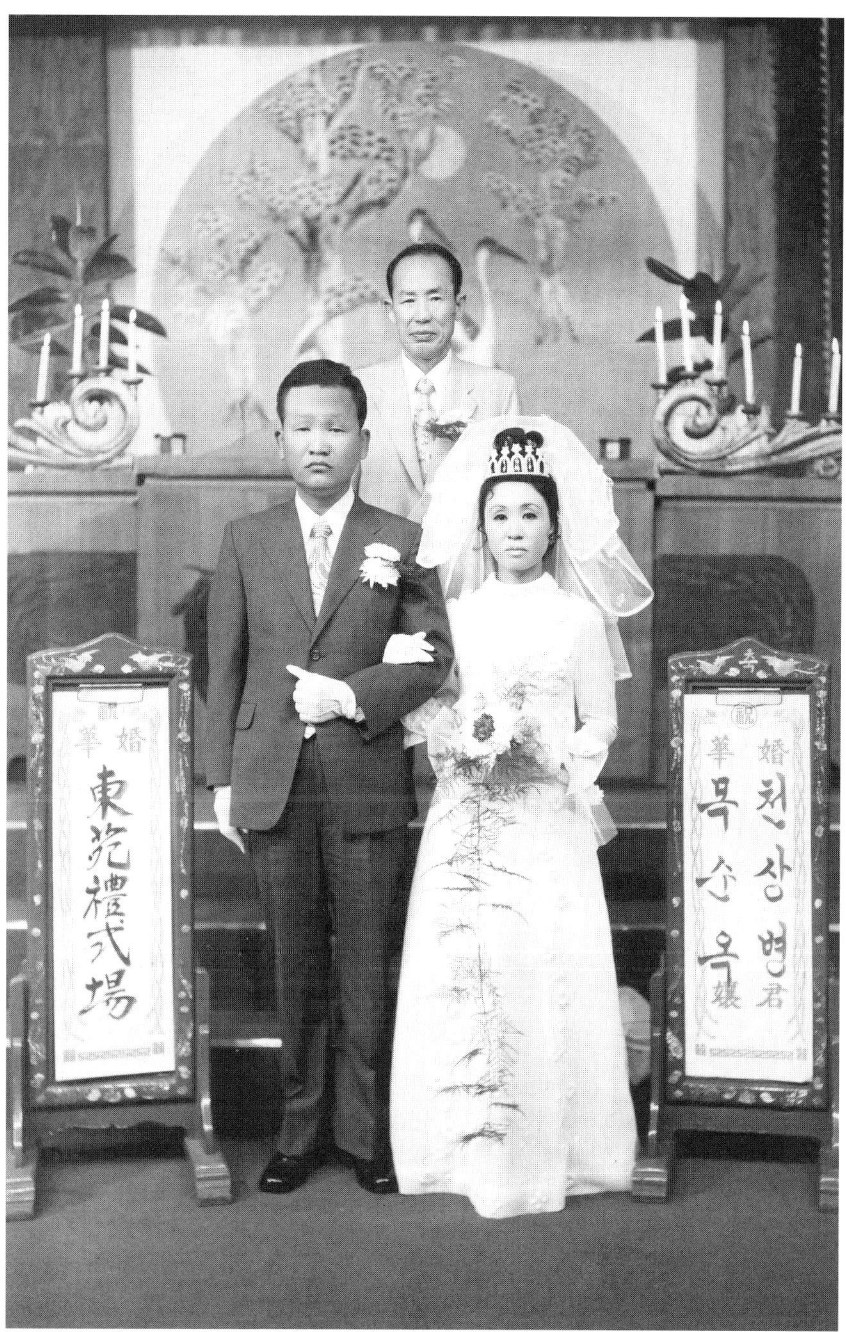


The poet Ch'ŏn Sang-pyŏng and his wife Mok Sun-ok on the day of their wedding.

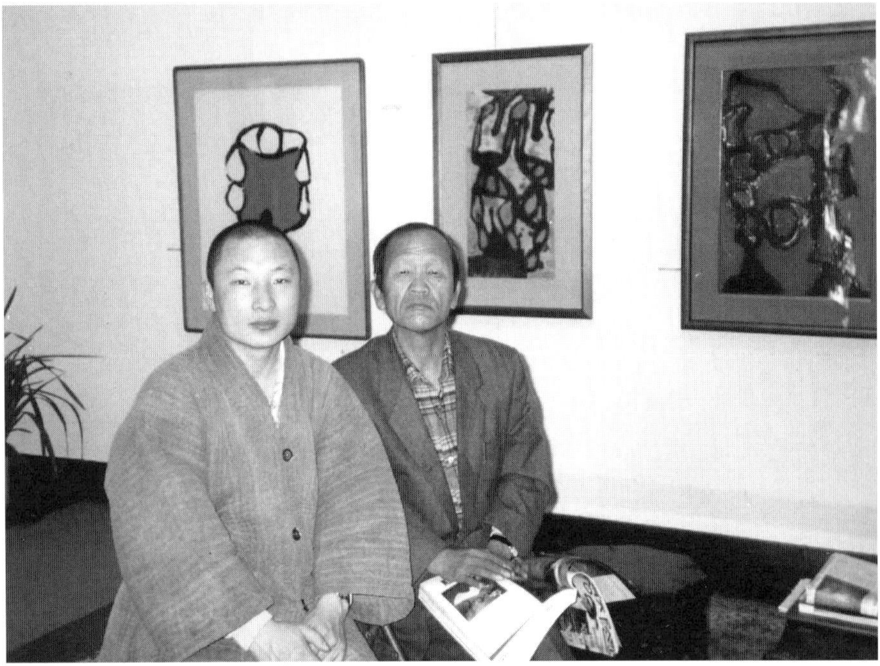

The poet with the artist-monk Sŏng-Yun Sunim, at the young monk's first exhibition.

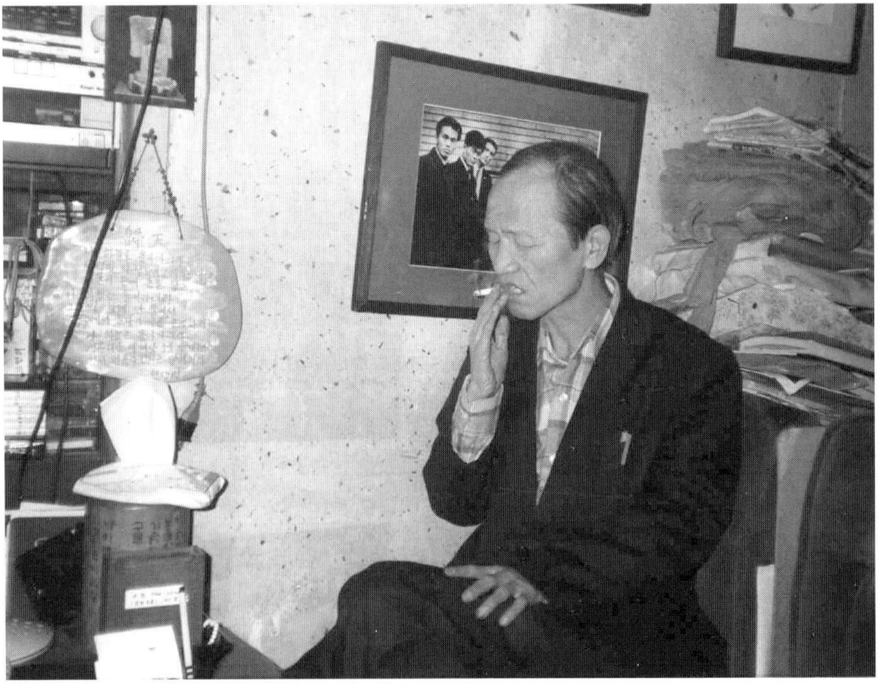

The poet engaged in another frequent activity, at his usual seat in Kwich'ŏn cafe in Insa-dong.

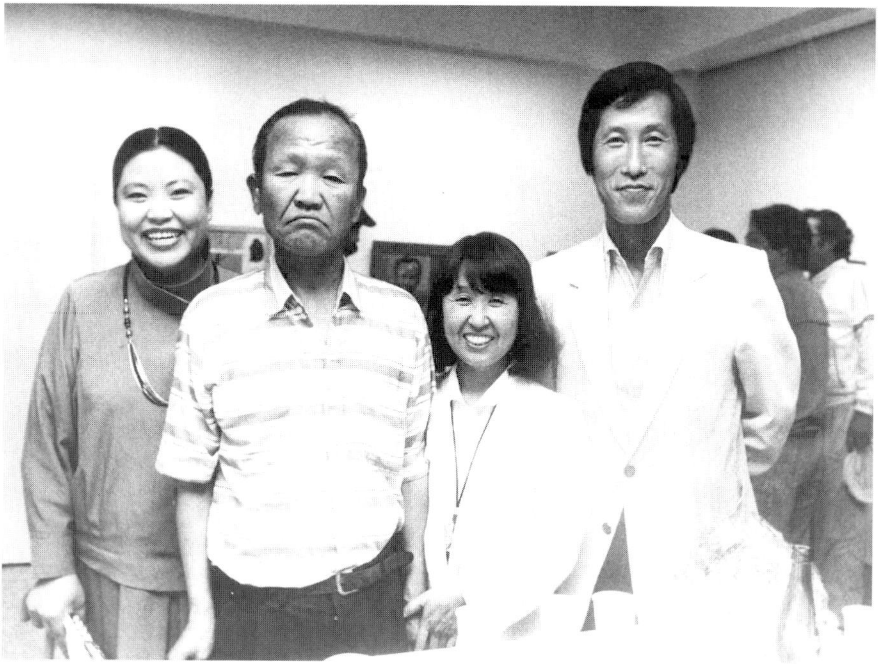

The poet with his wife and friends.

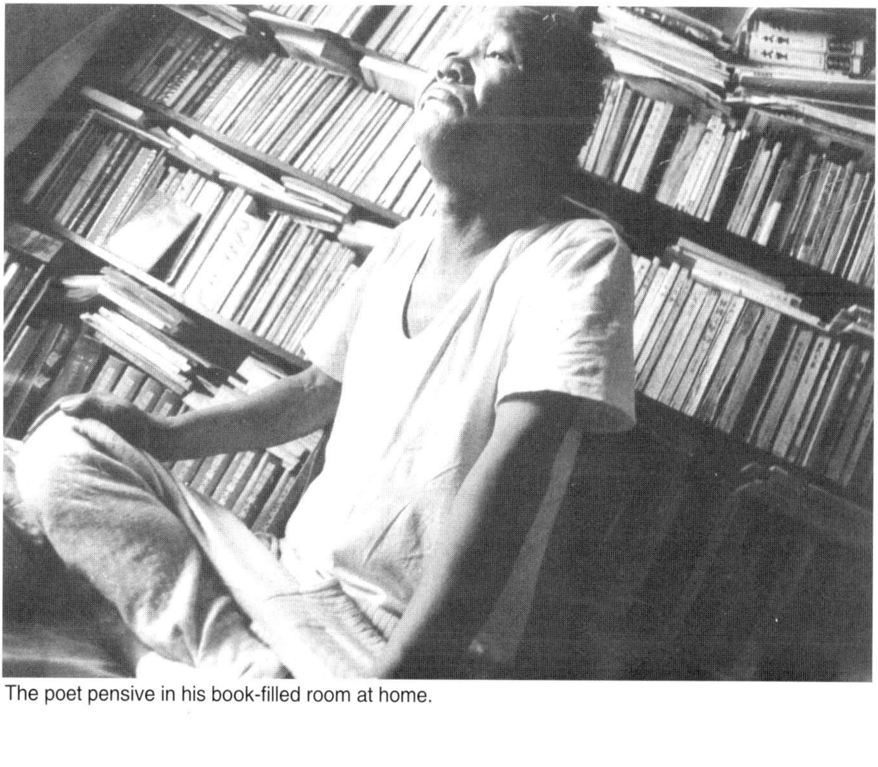

The poet pensive in his book-filled room at home.

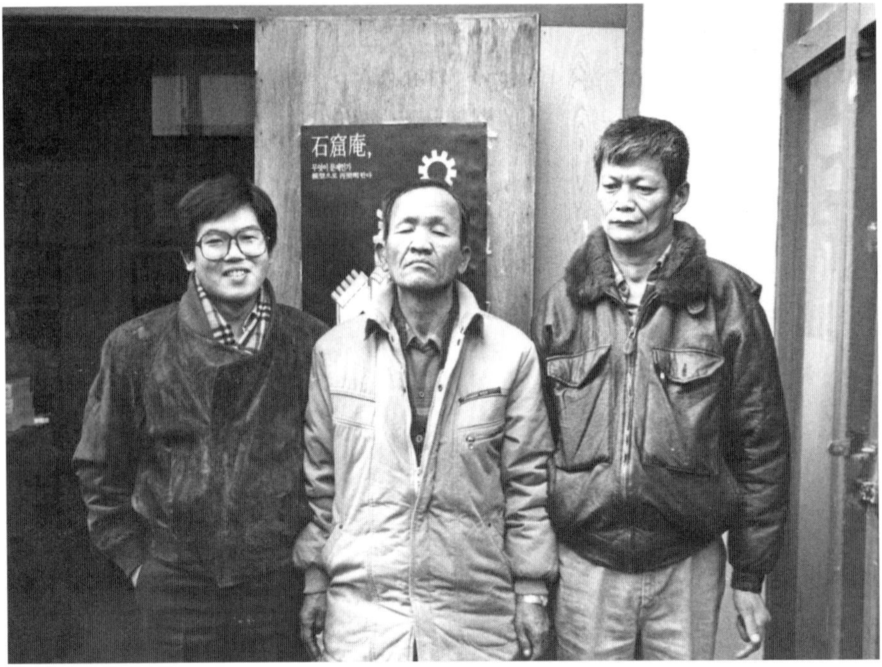

The poet with former school friends from Masan.

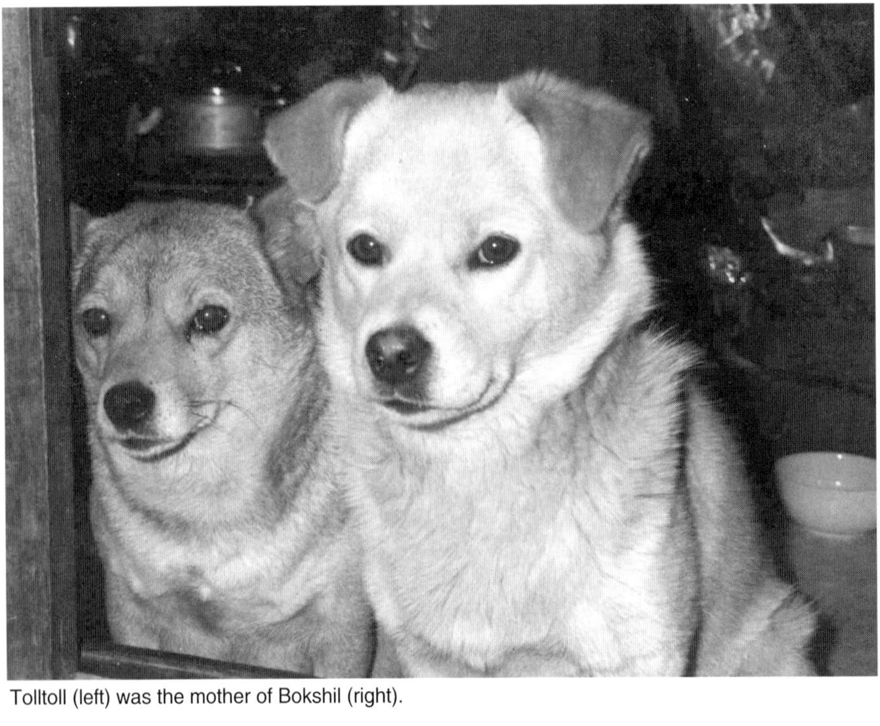

Tolltoll (left) was the mother of Bokshil (right).

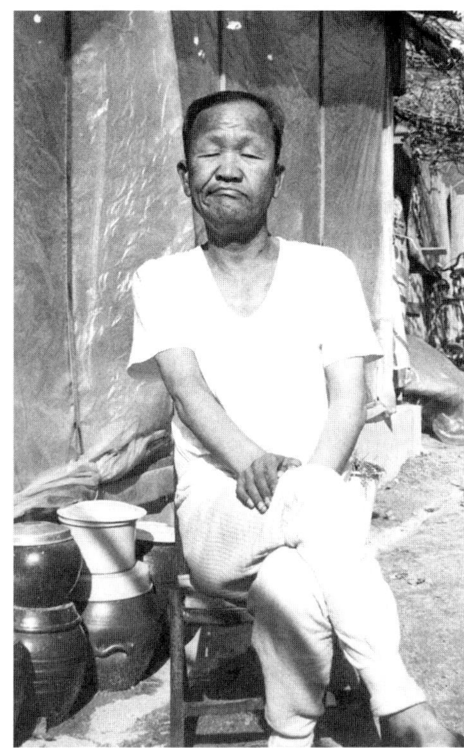
The poet at home outside Ŭijŏngbu.

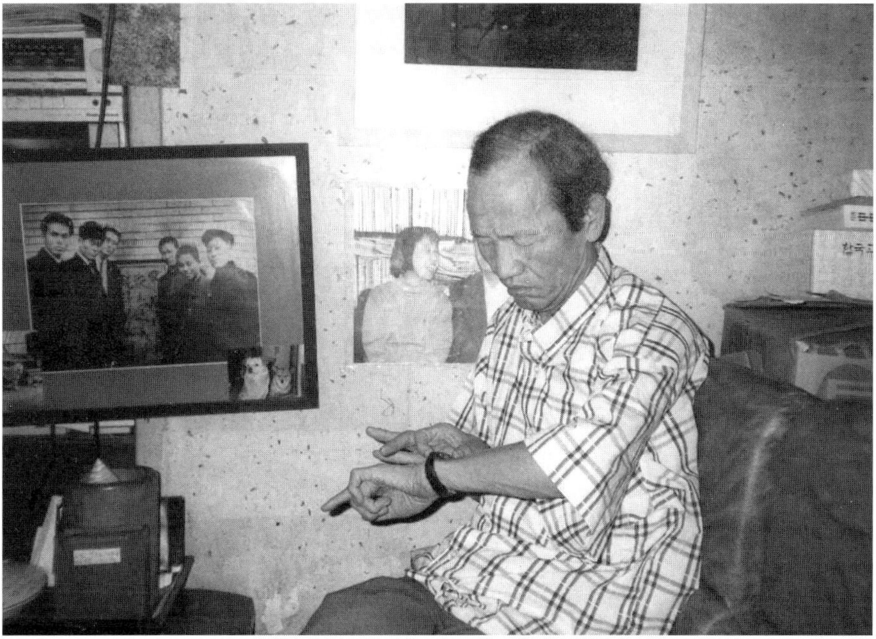

The poet consults his watch, as he so often did in his later years.

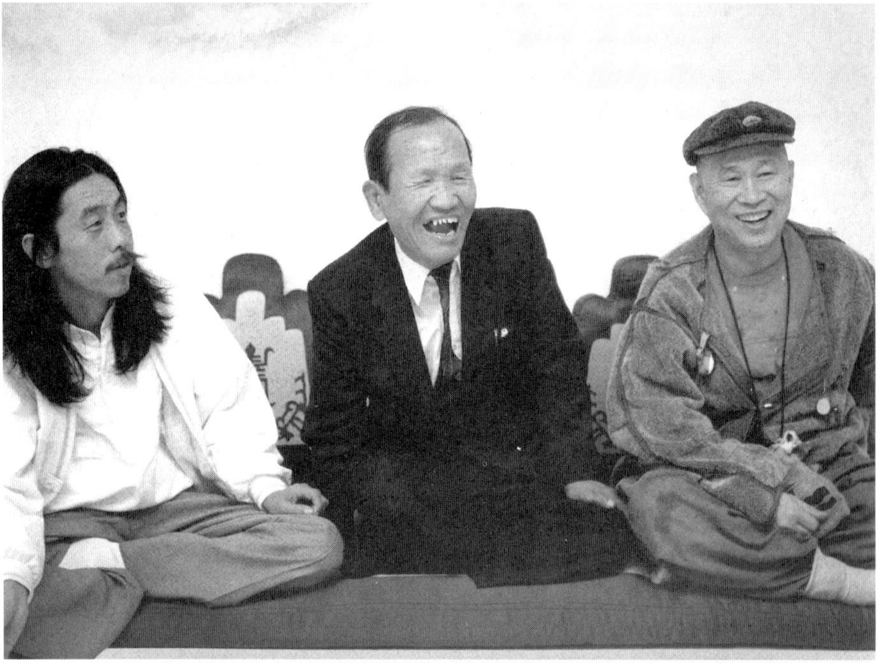

The “Three Bandits”: Lee Woi-su(left) and Chung Kwang the “Mad Monk” (right) with the poet.

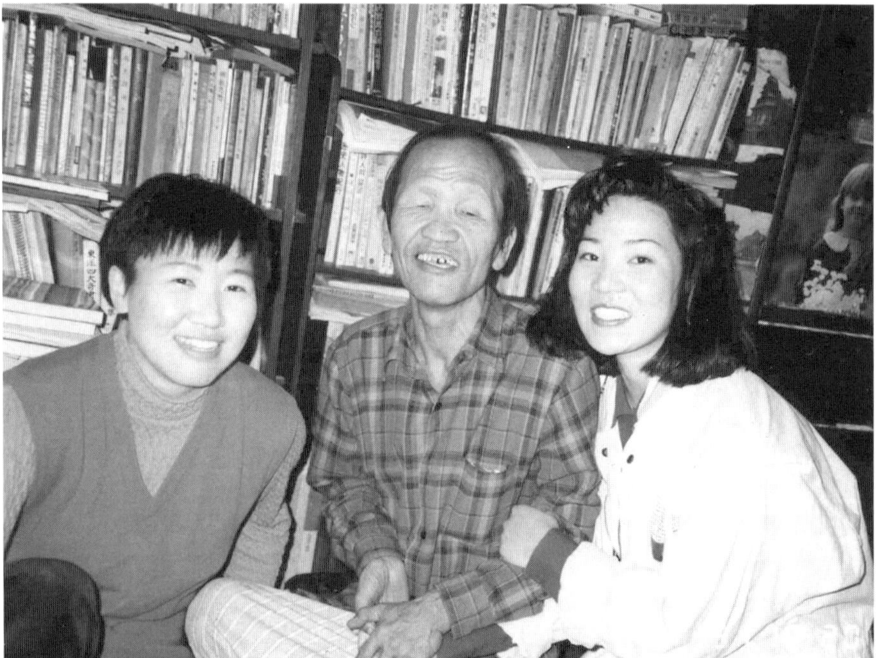

The poet in his room at home, welcoming admirers from a literary club.

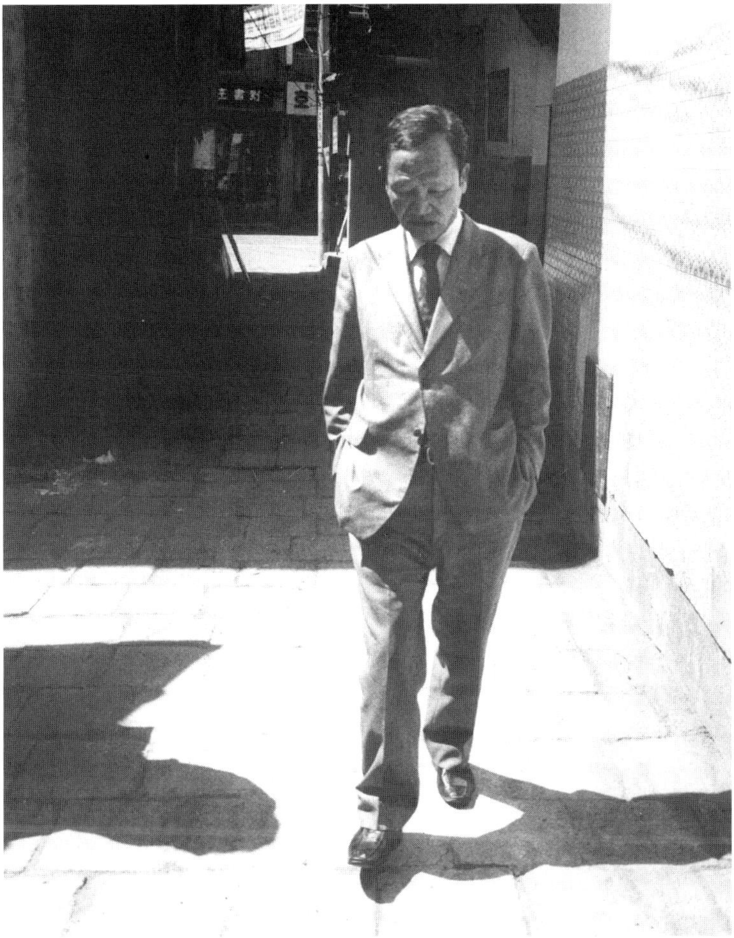

The poet walking to a formal event.

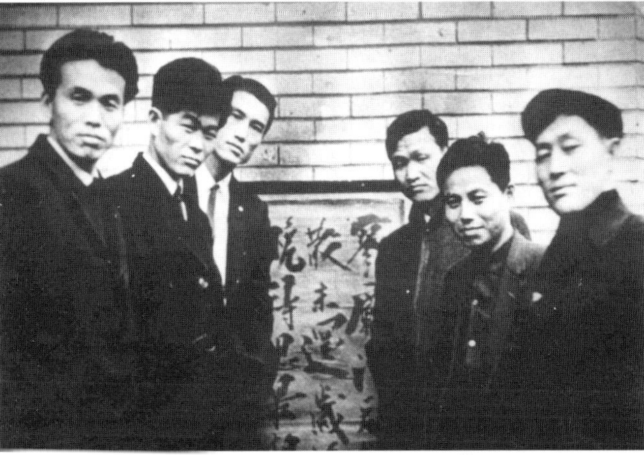

The poet as a Seoul National University student with a group of literary friends, most of whom also became writers.

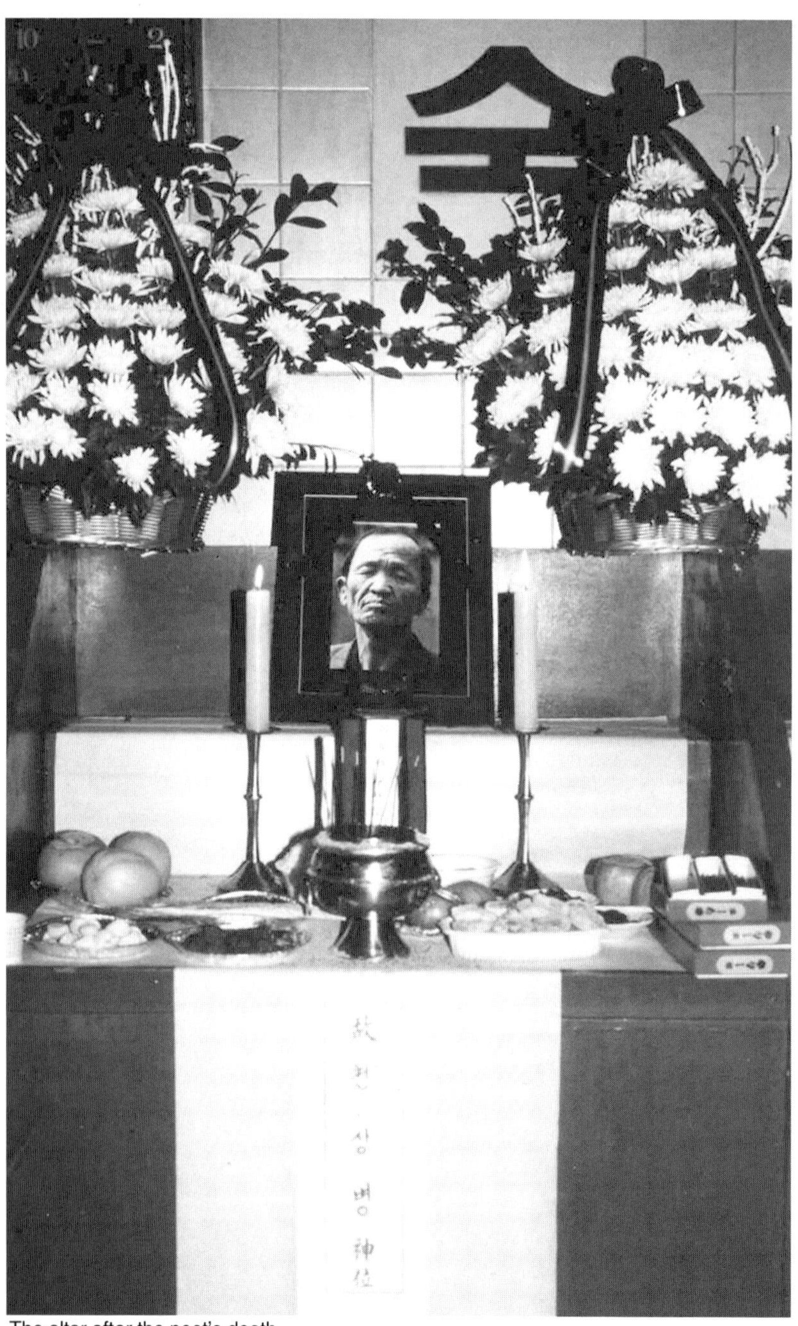


The altar after the poet’s death.